REVIEWS FOR DIRECTING 101

"On every college campus, there is always a "star" instructor, one whose classes are so well attended, students arrive 30 minutes early to get a seat. Ernest Pintoff is one of those teachers and his class is called Directing 101. This is a terrific book, and I am going to recommend it to all my students here at NYU."

> — David Irving,
> Acting Chair
> Graduate Film and Television Department
> New York University,
> Tish School of the Arts

"It's not far wrong to say that if you have digested Ernest Pintoff's remarkable book your only other needs as a director are talent, a story and a few dollars. *Directing 101* is amazingly thorough and, above all, practical. The author and his contributors are a treasury of what can be called inspirational good sense."

> — Charles Champlin
> Author of
> *George Lucas: The Creative Impulse*

"Ernest Pintoff's book is a very descriptive introductory guide through the entire filmmaking process. I recommend it!"
> — Elizabeth M. Daley
> Dean, USC School of Cinema/Television

DIRECTING 101

BY

ERNEST PINTOFF

based on his teachings at USC and UCLA

Published by Michael Wiese Productions, 11288 Ventura Blvd., Suite 821, Studio City, CA
91604, (818) 379-8799 Fax (818) 986-3408.
E-mail: wiese@earthlink.net
http://www.mwp.com

Cover design, photograph and illustrations by The Art Hotel
Interior design and layout by Gina Mansfield

Printed by McNaughton & Gunn, Inc., Saline, Michigan
Manufactured in the United States of America

The publisher plants two trees for every tree used in the manufacturing of this book. Printed
on recycled stock.

Library of Congress Cataloging in Publication Data

Pintoff, Ernest,
        Directing 101/ by Ernest Pintoff,
        p. cm.
        "Based on his teachings at USC and UCLA
        Includes bibliographical references and index.
        ISBN: 0-941188-67-1
        1. Motion pictures -- Production and direction.   I. Title.
PN1995.9.P7P52 1999
791.43'0233--dc21   97-51540
                                                                    CIP

DIRECTING 101

BY ERNEST PINTOFF

TABLE OF CONTENTS

PREFACE
by
Ernest Pintoff

In addition to film directing, probably the most enriching aspect of my career has been teaching. My intention with this book is to present a valuable source of filmmaking information and guidance to aspiring directors. As such, the contents reflect my film teaching experiences at both USC and UCLA.

While attending a liberal arts university, I received an M.F.A. in Art History. At the time, art was my passion. Now, I wish I had pursued a broader liberal arts education, concentrating on literature. As I hope you will glean from this book, the value of a broad-based foundation in literature is shared by many filmmakers. Elia Kazan said, "A film director is best equipped if he is well-read. He should study the classics for construction, exposition of theme, the means of characterization and for dramatic poetry."

My own hands-on introduction to filmmaking began as an apprentice animator at United Productions of America in California. A few years later, in 1955, I founded my own film studio in New York City, producing animated and live–action commercials as well as shorts. That led to an active period of directing numerous dramatic television films and several theatrical movies. Since 1973, I have also lectured and taught film directing and writing at the School of Visual Arts in New York, the University of Southern California School of Cinema and Television, the University of California at Los Angeles Extension, and the American Film Institute.

This book is written in the hope that my professional experience might enable me to contribute to the needs of today's aspiring filmmakers.

To offer multiple perspectives, I have invited a number of former and current students to express their views. I have also gathered observations and comments from film school graduates as well as professional filmmakers who evaluate their personal experiences and present their own advice. Their articles may be found following the text.

Looking back, I can say that it was my dad, a frustrated artist and musician, who was most influential in my becoming a filmmaker. A hard-working storekeeper and an affectionate father, he loved music and encouraged both my brother and me to play musical instruments. My father spoke frequently and fondly about our family roots in Poland as well as Latvia, and told us stories of his early adventures in America. Later, when he and I went to movies together, I began to notice the names of the art director on feature film credits, and dreamed of emulating them.

If you are a student, do not overlook the value of studying the humanities, history, and social sciences. Absorbing technical and production skills should only be part of your education. Read and write as much as possible. I believe that sensitivity to people as well as an awareness of society and the world is essential. A career in movies or television may be extremely rewarding both creatively and financially, but getting the right foundation is half the battle.

After completing your education, there are a number of ways to get started. There are no rules. You could write a screenplay or tele-play and submit that to an agent, producer, or successful television performer.

Studios and networks usually reject unagented scripts, primarily to avoid litigation in case they are developing a similar property along similar lines. Sometimes, however, a producer will consider an unsolicited piece because the quest for good material is always paramount. Fortunately, paper is relatively inexpensive, enabling one to continue writing during the struggle to get established.

As for getting a directing opportunity, a sample director's reel that demonstrates your skills as a filmmaker is what those in hiring positions mostly consider. Accordingly, I recommend that all aspiring filmmakers learn about the business aspects of movies and television. To expect to be presented with a plush, marketable assignment, no matter how talented you are, is naive. Experience and exposure of your work will help move you up the ladder, but the competition is fierce. I can attest to that.

During the course of this book, you will see that the position of the director is highly varied and complex. His or her work often is compared to that of the conductor of an orchestra or the captain of a ship. The film director is usually seen as the leader, providing a guiding force.

But the final outcome of the film is predetermined by the script, with the director providing both creative and organizational context.

There is little agreement among professional critics as to what exactly is the director's function. Some directors concentrate primarily on the structure of the script. Other directors are primarily occupied with the performance of actors. For them, the beauty of film correlates with the quality of acting. Those directors, among others, not only attend to acting performances as a whole, but to the many splendors of this wondrous medium.

ACKNOWLEDGMENTS

I would like to thank my colleagues as well as filmmakers and students who have contributed to this book, especially to Pat Richards for her fine research and editing. Alan Berger has been of valuable assistance as was Joseph Manduke for his good ideas and advice. I am also appreciative for the copyediting by Caroline Stack. Finally, I thank my wife, Caroline, for her support, affection, and numerous contributions.

Usually a renowned filmmaker would introduce a book such as this to readers. In this case, I asked Ray Greene, a former student, to write about his moviemaking experiences as well as the influence my directing course at the University of Southern California might have had on him. Presently, Greene is a film journalist and Editor-at-large of *Boxoffice Magazine*.

FOREWORD
by
Ray Greene

Back in the days when I was a graduate student, I had the good fortune to serve as a teaching assistant for similar courses by two very different directing instructors. One professor was the head of the University of Southern California cinema directing faculty, the other was Ernest Pintoff, and I found both their approaches to be incredibly instructive.

Obviously, there was a right way and a wrong way to make movies. From *Casablanca* to *City Lights* to *Weekend* and *Yellow Submarine*, a film made the right way might even manage to stir something deeper than our pleasure centers. But films made the wrong way so vastly outnumber the good stuff that there is no point in singling out a few by name. You want negative examples? Just turn on your television or make a hard right into a random movie house and chances are good you will find something dank and misshapen lying in wait for you, gnashing its teeth in the dark.

In contrast to my other professor, Pintoff was, and I'm sure still is, a nurturer. I assume that this has at least something to do with his eclectic background. The usual filmmaker is a monomaniac, whose interests run the gamut from movies to movies and back again. If he reads a novel, it is because his agent thinks that it might be a good property for him to adapt. If he ventures to a play, it's to check out a hot new actor, or to open negotiations with the writer for the screen rights before somebody else beats him to it.

It isn't that show folk are narrow-minded. In fact, some of the brightest people on the planet are bivouacking in Hollywood even as you read this, and that's been true going back as far as Ben Hecht's time. The reason most filmmakers are so focused is because what they do is so all-consuming. Be advised that there is no harder field to break into. Once you are inside or even halfway through the door, it's an ongoing tightrope act. Let's face it, just how many tightrope walkers find the time to pore over *Crime and Punishment*, as they juggle chain saws on that lonely wire?

Pintoff though, is a major exception to the monochromatic nature of most successful Hollywood filmmakers. In his long career, he has been a novelist as well as a screenwriter; a jazz musician who was good enough to play with the likes of Dexter Gordon; an academic who has shared his knowledge of the movie medium at some of the best film schools in the country; the writer, compiler, and editor of three oft-used works of nonfiction; and yes, Pintoff is one of the key figures in post-studio era movie animation, a graphic innovator with his own cult following.

What Pintoff seems to have gotten from his varied background is a deep understanding of the fact that there are many different paths to creative enlightenment. This is reflected in the way he views the choices of aspiring directors. Apparently, Pintoff operates from the belief that his students are working on their own way of seeing things. Like any swinging jazzman, he appreciates the director's need to improvise.

In filmmaking, we learn by doing and while we would all want to close our eyes and play some dazzling riffs, we've got to first practice our scales. So, pull up a chair, sit back, and listen to the maestro.

HOW MY CLASSES ARE CONDUCTED

Each of my three-hour directing classes is preceded by a brief review of what aspiring filmmakers are accomplishing, either positively or negatively. Then, two students are given exactly one hour to complete an adapted scene in class. I suggest that students adapt material from accomplished writers whose work has not already been visualized on film.

After each scene, I present my critique, then invite the class, as well as the actors, to critique their colleagues.

Although various aspects of directing are examined, special emphasis is placed on commitment, director's choice of material and acting. I do not permit students to utilize their own in-work or completed screenplays. It is suggested that my students adapt their screenplays from quality fiction writers such as Hemingway, Kafka, Poe, and Salinger.

I advocate that all scenes work in totality. They should have a beginning, middle, and end.

Playwrights whose work is suggested for adaptation are Edward Albee, Sholem Aleichem, Samuel Beckett, Bertolt Brecht, Paddy Chayevsky, Bruce Jay Friedman, Herb Gardner, Lorraine Hansberry, Lillian Hellman, Israel Horovitz, Langston Hughes, Eugene Ionesco, Claude Van Italie, Leroi Jones, Arthur Kopit, Claire Booth Luce, David Mamet, Terrence McNally, Arthur Miller, Clifford Odets, Eugene O'Neil, John Osborne, Harold Pinter, Luigi Pirandello, Murray Schisgal, Peter Shaffer, Sam Sheppard, Tom Stoppard, and Wendy Wasserstein.

I urge my students to avoid proscenium staging and to conceive of their scenes from within a natural environment, not from a theater audience *point of view*, striving to achieve cinematic acting that is real. Props and wardrobe should also look as realistic as possible.

I remind students that although my course is a directing class, the choice of material and quality of the adaptation and writing will also be scrutinized. I also explain that my critiques may be very personal, and that I will comment on the students' behavior on set as well as their demeanor.

At least one week prior to production, student directors present their scenarios to me, including a single-paragraph synopsis of the intended scene. At this point, I stress the significance of having the opportunity to choose quality material and to direct it relatively free of supervision.

I also emphasize the importance of casting, and that it is essential to direct material with which they are familiar. Mostly, I urge students to select material with which they have an emotional bond and connection. I believe that it is essential, on the other hand, to remain at an emotional distance from cast and crew when filming.

Actor Al Pacino, in an interview with film students, remarked that the relationship with other cast members is a delicate one. "Once, I fell deeply in love with my female lead during the shoot, then had to struggle to remain distant because, paradoxically, it was marring my on-screen performance."

SELECTING AND ACQUIRING MATERIAL

First, you should have a strong emotional connection with your material.

Since I believe that the material you choose is even more important than the craft of directing, do not settle for mediocrity. The director's task is difficult enough. Quality material is crucial for success. Of course, you should have a knack for determining just what the concept of quality entails. Often, this becomes quite a personal decision.

Director Howard Hawks said, "I don't think plot really means much. I'd say that everybody has seen every plot twenty times. What they haven't seen is characters and their relation to one another. I don't worry about plot."

Renowned French director Jean Renoir, during the filming of *Grand Illusion* in 1937, said, "Movies are not reality, especially if you can find a better seat in a café on the Champs Elysées. You can find reality when you watch people and hear them speaking. But when you are making a movie, you must be imaginative." So, who you are as an individual will help determine what kind of material appeals to you.

You should also give practical consideration to both the final budget and market for the film. For example, period pieces or stories with many locations, characters, stunts, and special effects are obviously costly, so these projects are most likely to be produced and released by major film companies. Trying to do justice to such a tale without the necessary means can only bring frustration, no matter how much you are fascinated by the subject.

3

Should you choose a short piece of fiction or novel that you would like to adapt for film or free and pay-television, rights and permission to use the material must first be legally obtained. These are usually negotiated with either the original author or publisher or their representative.

Contact may be made by phone or in writing to determine if the property is available for development in all media, including movies, free and pay-television, radio, and further optioning.

One may ask how a movie budgeted for $7.5 million dollars ends up costing $36 million. Former worldwide head of United Artists, Steven Bach, reveals in his book *Final Cut*, that it's not all that difficult, as he writes about director Michael Camino's 1980 infamous production of *Heaven's Gate*. I heartily recommend Bach's cautionary tale to all aspiring filmmakers.

Most producers and major film companies concerned with lawsuits of plagiarism and rights require independent sources submitting material either to sign a release form or else have the project submitted by an authorized agent before they will even give it consideration.

Acquiring classic material or stories in the public domain should always be checked through the U.S. Copyright Office in Washington, D.C. If available, acquiring these rights should not be a problem. But understand that your rights are not exclusive.

Next, the fee for acquisition is determined. This may be accomplished by negotiating option periods by increments, percentages, buy-outs, or a combination thereof.

In some cases, the original author may wish to participate creatively or be involved in the production. It would therefore be necessary to specify this in contract form.

I strongly advise that you do not start working or writing until formal legal agreements are executed, and recommend that an attorney be consulted before finalizing matters.

Despite any legal or financial difficulties, the use of classic material is very often a wise artistic choice. Fortunately, much classic material is solidly structured, gripping, and multilayered or it would not have endured. I am speaking here of writers such as Shakespeare, Poe, or Hugo. On the other hand, you must be able to judge whether or not your classic story can be made relevant for today's audiences. *Romeo and Juliet* was originally written for the stage, but has been subsequently adapted for the screen more than once. No doubt the drama will continue to attract many directors in the future.

Others have chosen to capitalize on television nostalgia by bringing fresh movie life to such varied small-screen fare as "Star Trek," "The Brady Bunch," and "Mission Impossible." With such popular material, the quality of instant recognition is a powerful draw. But with that comes an unusually high degree of expectation. So, if you do choose such material, be prepared for a possible backlash.

After reflection, one might conclude that it is easier and more economical to create your own screenplay or teleplay.

Should you choose to write an original screenplay, I suggest that you first synopsize your idea in one short paragraph. At that stage, you may best analyze the story structure. It should be pointed out that the most successful and enduring stories, those that have become classics over the years, frequently contain a strong social component.

A one-paragraph synopsis usually tells how we get from the beginning, through the middle and to the conclusion of a story. For example, *One Flew Over the Cuckoo's Nest* is about a mental asylum inmate who battles the will of a sadistic nurse until she and the system win.

Screenplays such as *Chinatown* by Robert Towne, *Schindler's List* by Steven Zallian, and *The Godfather* by Francis Ford Coppola and Mario Puzo are not only solidly structured with unique and memorable characters but also make profound economic, social, and political statements. Story qualities that usually elevate writing above the mundane involve highly charged situations such as life and death confrontations, intense familial conflicts, and the dynamics of revenge. Shakespeare employed these themes in almost all of his tragic works.

The Godfather, with such elements of Greek tragedy as hubris, fratricide, and fate, hints darkly that crime does not pay because of the ultimate sacrifice of any personal and family life.

Next, expand your concept to a full outline, and then to a completed script. Screenplay page lengths vary. One page generally translates to one screen minute. Therefore a screenplay of approximately 120 pages would equate to a typical full-length feature film. It is recommended that your screenplay writing style follow the industry standard format and be entered and saved on computer. Proper examples of script formatting may be found in *The Complete Guide to Standard Script Formats* by Hillis Cole and Judith Haag.

A similar work approach should hold true in collaborating with another screenwriter. Since it is essential that clear communication be established between collaborators, each writer should prepare a separate synopsis for comparison and agreement before launching into writing the outline and screenplay together.

Should a director decide to have his original idea executed by a professional writer into a screenplay, it is essential that a mutual understanding be established. The same creative and business guidelines as previously described should be maintained. That is, have the writer deliver his work in increments: first, the one paragraph summary, then the outline, and finally the completed script. Also, have formal legal written agreements drawn up.

The following is a sample of a basic business agreement between director and writer, if cowriting:

"This confirms that both parties shall share in writing credits and fees as well as creative decisions pertaining to the screenplay, to be approximately 120 pages in length.

"Completion date of the screenplay shall be mutually agreed upon, and should either party fail to perform, all rights would revert to the original creator of the idea.

"Should it become necessary to involve the services of another writer in the project, the writers shall renegotiate in good faith regarding fees and credits."

Writers may protect any written creative work by simply sending the document in a self-addressed envelope to oneself by registered mail. The Writers Guild Of America (WGA) will also record the content and date of a work for anyone, even nonmembers, at a nominal charge.

The following is a sample of a basic agreement between the purchaser and writer of original fictional material:

"The writer does not authorize or permit anyone other than the purchaser to use, in connection with any film or free and pay-television or radio program, any of the fictional characters who appear in the property. Further, the writer represents that he has not previously authorized anyone other than the purchaser to use any of these characters in connection with any film or free and pay-television or radio program.

"The writer shall also receive screen credit substantially as follows: Based on the original work by the author.

"Should this film be distributed for exhibition or for free and pay-television, the purchaser shall pay the writer a percentage of the purchaser's net profits from distribution."

The preceding samples are merely key points to be observed and individually negotiated. An attorney should prepare the final agreement.

As an exercise, try writing your own basic legal agreement or understanding. This can be good practice for clear writing and analysis which could potentially reduce legal fees.

Standard sample legal contracts, which probably will need to be amended, are obtainable from many stationery stores. Of course, unusually intricate contracts should be drafted by a skilled attorney.

Finally, it is my opinion that too many students needlessly fear their ideas may be stolen. General ideas cannot be protected by copyright. So, have confidence in your ability to create, and express yourself freely.

BUDGETING AND FINANCING

After the script is completed, the director becomes involved in the film's budget and then the often difficult matter of financing.

If you are a first-time director, you might contact foundations, government agencies, private corporations, television stations and festivals, all of which may offer financing specifically for the production of a film. A list of international film festivals is available from the Academy of Motion Picture Arts and Sciences.

A significant source of financing is through foundations. Some excellent low-budget films have been made using grant money. There are several useful books available that cover the topic of foundation grants, and a reference librarian should be able to lead you to the most current and comprehensive of these. In addition, if you are fortunate enough to obtain a good agent, he or she should be able to help you gain consideration for a low-budget film project.

The budget, script analysis, and breakdown for production are usually accomplished by the unit production manager (UPM) in consultation with the director and producer.

Each scene is analyzed by indicating location, day or night shooting, actors, minor-aged actors, nonspeaking actors, animals, extras, vehicles, special effects, and stunts. This information is recorded on thin separate strips of cardboard. Then, the production team juggles and places the strips onto what is called a production board. Before tabulating the budget, each strip is evaluated for production practicality and cost while considering the director's preference of shooting order. When the budget is finalized, it is approved by the director, as stipulated by the Directors Guild of America (DGA).

Occasionally, certain valuable cast and crew members are compensated with additional money beyond basic Guild minimums. The director, the original author of the material, and the screenwriter may each receive approximately 5 percent of the total shooting budget. In some cases, other key personnel may be equally rewarded. However, a popular star has no limit to his financial arrangement.

In order to understand how these participation deals work, it is important to know that gross profits are defined as being the full amount of money earned by a film's distribution before expenses have been deducted. Net profits are the amount of money remaining from the gross receipts after negative costs, distribution, deferments, and profit participations have been deducted.

Fees for the acquisition of rights, directing, writing, cast, producing, and composing are generally referred to as *above–the–line* expenditures. *Below–the–line* items constitute day-to-day costs, including crew fees, equipment, editing, postproduction, sound, music production, vehicles, transportation, office and medical expenses, insurance, and legal and accounting fees.

As a rule, the production budget reflects the total approximate film costs. Traditionally, it comprises one third for preproduction, one third for actual filming, and one third for postproduction.

Sometimes the actual timeframe of filmmaking works out the same way. After the making of *Lawrence of Arabia*, director David Lean said, "I spent one year in working with the writer and preproduction, one year filming and one year in postproduction."

In short, directors acquire production financing for filming and development in a number of ways. The script, cast, key personnel, and marketing potentials are the main ingredients a backer evaluates. Independent financing is most desirable, in that it usually provides the director with the greatest control and creative freedom.

Funding is also available for film or free and pay-television by major film studios, but those sources frequently maintain cast and various other controls that often limit the director's autonomy. But, when starting your career, you may need to compromise to get your film made at all. Regarding an established financing source, Woody Allen stated, "They gave me total control over what necktie I could wear while directing. So, I went ahead with the movie." In reality, Allen is content to continue making relatively low-budget films.

CASTING AND COMMUNICATING WITH ACTORS

One of the most significant decisions for the film director is choosing the right cast. As with the selection of material, this too is personal and emotional.

Should you have the budget for a casting director, it is important that he or she be thoroughly familiar with the screenplay and characters. The casting director not only provides the director with photographs of actors, samples of their work, and knowledge of acting credits, but is usually first to contact the actor or actor's agent and arrange for the meeting or audition with the director.

Negotiations regarding fees and scheduling are also handled by the casting director within budget parameters. Professional actors as well as extras are members of the Screen Actors Guild in New York, Chicago, and Hollywood and the Guild will provide agency contact information about all members. Industry publications such as *Dramalogue* are also useful in attracting talent to your audition.

The administrative procedures in casting vary according to the producing set-up, the film, the location, and the producer–director relationship. Furthermore, the parts that the actors fill are generally classified as leads, supporting players, bit parts, and extras. In Hollywood, where type-casting is prevalent, this is often the key factor in the selection of a film actor. To further handle the exigencies of production in Los Angeles, there exists a Central Casting Corporation, which has listings of all the various and special types of actors and serves as a clearinghouse for the major studios. In most other cities, the agents themselves perform this role. In some situations, the producer may wish to contact an actor directly.

Since the New York Screen Actors Guild is associated with the West Coast actors' and extras' guilds through the Associated Actors and Artists of America, there is little difference between the East Coast and West Coast as far as union regulations are concerned. Throughout all sections of the country, actors secure work through agents who function somewhat like employment agencies and are paid by the actors.

Auditions and meetings are conducted by directors in various ways. Essentially, it is important to realize that the actor is indeed interested in winning the part. So, when he appears, sometimes even dressed as the character, the actor is understandably anxious and nervous. It is therefore the director's responsibility to keep conditions comfortable and creatively interesting. This, incidentally, is no different than the atmosphere the director must maintain during filming.

The director inevitably takes the credit or blame for everything that is good or bad in a film, including the acting. Should the actor do something poorly, then the director may have to say something like "That's not good. Shall we try another one?" Or the director could say, "That was excellent! Shall we try another one?"

Film-actor-turned-director Sidney Poitier said that he became distraught when a director provided the most intimate acting criticism to him in front of the cast and crew. "When I direct, I call actors aside and speak to them in strictly private terms," said Poitier.

Concerning keeping the actors comfortable, I have noticed that neophyte and shy student directors tend to spend an inordinate amount of time actually directing the actors and crew from a monitor that is not within their view or peripheral vision. I therefore encourage students to stay close to the action on set, as everyone thrives on the director remaining nearby.

All decisions and responsibilities are ultimately the director's. As with all aspects of directing, it is important to open and maintain free communication with actors from the onset.

Today, many professional actors still use the method technique, approaching their characterizations instinctively and nonintellectually. Renowned Russian acting teacher Konstantin Stanislovsky said, "The actor must draw from private experiences and feelings and thus become the character. The style of acting will therefore be extremely natural. Performances can then be low-keyed, with pauses, hesitations and gropings for meaning and communication." Some method-trained actors hired for small-screen work have initial difficulty working in what is often a fast-paced environment and must adapt their preparation techniques accordingly.

The chief American proponents of the Stanislovsky technique were Harold Clurman and Lee Strasberg, who established the Actor's Studio in New York City. In addition to nurturing and spawning countless actors such as Marlon Brando, Geraldine Page, and Paul Newman, the Studio also provided the foundation for playwrights such as Arthur Miller, Tennessee Williams, Neil Simon, and film directors Elia Kazan, John Frankenheimer, and Gene Wilder.

When I studied directing at the Actor's Studio, I soon realized how intensely a performer must concentrate to effect a truly private moment. This unique moment occurs when the character is totally aware that he can express any part of himself. It could be represented even by such an innocuous incident as scratching oneself, supposedly unobserved. Film audiences like to eavesdrop on these private moments.

Playwrights of stature, such as Arthur Miller, insist on retaining their dialogue as originally written. For example, when Dustin Hoffman wanted to improvise in the television version of *Death of a Salesman*, he and Miller clashed.

Whatever style actors may use, most are capable of improvisation. Using that technique during the casting interview could possibly be the quickest and surest way to evaluate talent.

As a former animator switching to live-action directing, I was particularly drawn to using improvisation when filming. Actually, improvisation is often used in live-action picture making on many levels. Employing improvisation during actual filmmaking can be exhilarating, especially when one is used to working under the constraints of frame by frame animation. But if you become seduced by such a working method, be warned. Your spontaneously created universe may turn out to be either wildly fascinating or boring.

Almost without exception, the best directors are familiar with many acting techniques and approaches and have studied acting themselves. It is most important to be able to explain, if necessary, the meaning of subtext to actors, that is, the motivations, emotions, and ideas residing beneath the surface text. The subtext is implicit and adds subtlety, resonance and excitement to an actor's work.

To promote unpredictability in an actor's performance, I employ exercises that will hopefully reduce the use of clichés. For example, rather than smiling after tasting a delectable bite of food or sniffing a pleasurable scent, it could be more natural to project an aura of seriousness and immersion in the senses. There are a great variety of exercises that a director may use, both when casting and preparing a scene, to break the tension as well as to illuminate the participants' particular talents. These exercises may be invented by the director or gleaned from any actor's handbook on improvisation.

Believe it or not, I have directed both feature and television actors, who, when moving forward to kiss, try positioning themselves to the camera in such a way that they will be featured most favorably. One must be extremely careful when working with such talent, who in their motions are motivated more by ego or insecurity than by the needs of the role. Obviously it is most important for the actor to move naturally. Traditionally, the great male stars of the past such as Spencer Tracy, Humphrey Bogart, and James Cagney courteously deferred to their female costars' movements while managing to appear totally natural.

Be prepared to read the script or improvise with auditioning actors. If possible, it is best to have actors audition or read together. Also, be careful not to prejudge the original concept of the character. Select the best, most exciting and interesting actor, remaining open to new perceptions regarding gender as well as race.

Unlike cinema actors, those who have been theatrically trained may tend to overplay emotions since they are used to projecting to live audiences. And since film scenes are seldom shot in the order of their appearance, a performer who has worked extensively in the theater may have problems because he cannot rely on audience reaction. The very unity of his performance must be mental. The role of a good director comes into play here, because an actor in a screen role may need to depend far more on a director than he does in the theater.

Depending on the type of film you are making, you might want to consider a novice actor or actress or even a nonactor. Directors such as Vittorio De Sica, Elia Kazan, and Federico Fellini have used untrained actors most effectively.

Cinema acting requires extraordinary subtleties in listening, speaking, and reacting because the camera and screen provide the audience with close-up perspectives. Film sound and stock are extremely sensitive, picking up the slightest mutterings and murmurs, as well as the smallest eye, mouth, and postural movements.

On her view of film acting, Katherine Hepburn facetiously remarked, "After all, acting in front of a camera is a minor art. Shirley Temple has been doing it since she was four."

Once, when I was filming an actor playing an insecure character, he refused to make eye contact with the other actor in a particular scene, although it was called for in the script. When shooting, I have always tried to respect the actor's choices, especially when they are reasonable.

A happy cast and crew usually reflect a smoothly running shoot, which conse-quently affects both the overall quality and cost of production.

Regarding makeup, I do not encourage its heavy use, as the camera is sure to detect it. I prefer casting to type and

directing large crew in Oregon

age, rather than having actors hide behind makeup. Hairpieces and hair coloring should be another concern, because they too are usual-ly obvious on screen.

Beware of your talent's possible vanity, as you do not want the audience distracted by artificial details which may be annoying, such as a boom microphone becoming visible. During class filming, I have witnessed an inexperienced actor, when the director called for an extreme close-up, shout in a rather panicked way, "Makeup!" Besides being a bit hammy, the request is also inappropriate in my opinion because the same appearance for the actor ideally should be maintained in all camera angles.

It is sometimes difficult for a theatrically trained actor to give up the security of heavy makeup or hairpieces, especially when he is not used to having a camera zoom into his face with the intention of showing a vastly enlarged, permanent image of it to millions of viewers.

18

Be sensitive to such concerns by promoting a relaxed atmosphere on set. When filming an intimate scene or any other highly personal or difficult scene, the mood on set is foremost. It is natural for actors to exhibit some self-consciousness in certain instances and you as the director must do everything possible to promote a comfortable, professional, and sensitive atmosphere. Keep the set clear of all those who are not absolutely necessary.

Acting in cinema is not at all similar to theatrical skills. I look for explosive or nonpredictable qualities in all performances. It is also useful during auditions to listen carefully to the reading and look into the eyes of the performer. Should you notice a marked liveliness there, instead of an opaqueness or listlessness, you should likely give that actor strong consideration. Director Howard Hawks, when asked to name the most important element in an actor's performance, had a one-word response: Confidence.

The role of an effective performer is to make the audience comfortable with the character he is playing. He must gain the audience's trust and keep it.

In filmmaking, the actor's concentration is paramount. As director, you should be aware that acting on a quiet film set without the spontaneous reaction of a live audience is difficult. Be supportive and welcome an actor's input. At the same time, technical requirements might hinder the theater actor. For example, the screen actor must often remember to tilt his head in a certain way to avoid a light or prop. When there is camera movement, he must time his actions so that the grips, the camera operator, and other actors may time their respective movements.

Many actors like to prepare for their roles by researching related real characters and writing their biographies. They may also scour thrift shops to find certain key props and to select pieces of wardrobe. Sally Field, John Travolta, and other actors have stated they quite often get that initial spark they need to begin fleshing out a character through

19

finding a particular article of clothing. On the other hand, when doing a period piece, you must be careful that your actors are not so influenced by unusual apparel that they overact or otherwise behave in an artificial manner. Director Paul Thomas Anderson, speaking about the filming of his *Boogie Nights*, revealed that he was terribly worried his characters would begin hamming it up outrageously once in their form-fitting polyester suits of the 1970s, and so he warned them accordingly.

In addition, directors should inform the actor not to radically change hair and makeup without first consulting them. Finally, if time, cost, and conditions permit, it is prudent to produce a screen test. You will find that even major stars who want a choice role will willingly submit to a test.

I consider the casting of extras and nonspeaking roles almost as important as casting the principal parts. Although this is often arranged by the casting director, I suggest that the director approve those selections. When dealing with many extras, some directors find it logistically useful to assign roles for them, even though some of the choices may never come to light on screen. For example, when shooting *Dog Day Afternoon*, Sidney Lumet had an outdoor crowd broken down into individual characters: sixteen protesters, six teenagers playing hooky, and four truck drivers. Each extra was given a name as well as a detailed diagram of the set as he arrived on the scene so that he knew precisely what to do.

An amusing and effective use of extras occurred for the filming of *Ben Hur* in 1926. Special effects men not only built a full-sized set of the Circus Maximus in ancient Rome, but also a model that would reduce the need for extras. This model included silhouettes of thousands of spectators made of wood that could leap to their feet and wave their arms mechanically.

In summary, I believe that the best directors know how to provide actors with a creative and comfortable working atmosphere.

CREW SELECTION

The producer, director, and production manager usually select the key members of the crew. These decisions are based on technical requirements, budget, and personal preference. Once you have chosen the key personnel, the job of crewing is complete, for each of these people will bring his own support staff as determined by necessity and budget.

The key people on most crews are the *cinematographer, first assistant director, film editor, sound mixer, gaffer, key grip, production designer, property master, wardrobe master, key makeup artist, special-effects expert, stunt coordinator* or *gaffer, location manager, unit production manager (UPM), still photographer,* and *set construction foreman.*

The film director usually concentrates on actors and action, whereas the cinematographer focuses on the picture and lighting. Academy Award winning cinematographer James Wong Howe said, "I find it most difficult to find a director who is truly sensitive to the needs of the cinematographer." A smart director will appreciate the special skills of his or her cinematographer, for in the end, the look and feel of a film may well be the most indelible and enduring aspect of the entire project. The award-winning documentary *Visions of Light* is well worth watching for its glimpse into the working techniques and approaches of various notable cinematographers, both past and present.

Possibly the most important crew member on the film director's team is the first assistant director (AD). This choice, as backed up by the DGA contract, is strictly the director's, as it should be, because the AD can be the director's greatest ally, confidant, and helper.

21

It is essential that the AD be apprised of all plans. Ideally, that includes both the director's creative and production intentions. Being able to share these ideas with your AD should be invaluable, since not only will the AD know where your creative values lie, but he may function as the liaison with the producer, cinematographer, UPM, cast, and departmental heads.

Professional ADs are almost always members of the DGA. They go through a rigorous application and apprentice procedure although they are not necessarily intent upon becoming directors. In fact, Guild rules state that the AD may not take over for the director during the production on which he is currently working. But the AD may leave the production should he be offered an assignment as director on another film.

In addition to communicating with cast and crew, including the production designer and director of photography, the assistant director is an immeasurable aid during the production when scheduling time is critical.

The AD, knowing when and where the camera will be positioned, may become involved in decisions concerning set construction. He will report to the UPM, who in turn communicates with teamsters when shooting on location, to determine where production vehicles should be parked so that they are out of picture range.

The director of photography (DP), is the person next in line with whom the AD will work closely. That includes following up on ordering equipment and scheduling. The second AD is the AD's main helper. He usually issues the call sheets and notifies the cast and crew where and when to appear for work.

Two preconceived notions that I would like to dispel are that producers are only primarily concerned with budgets and profits. It is my opinion that many producers are well read, creative, and articulate and

22

it is up to the director to establish an amicable and productive relationship. That same attitude extends to working with the writer, both on and off the set. Unfortunately, association with the writer has been traditionally unwelcome by directors during production. But I strongly recommend keeping in close communication at all times.

Concerning his relationship with screenwriters, the esteemed director George Cukor said, "I am very dependent upon writers. There is an old theatrical saying that claims when a scene is well-written, it will play itself. I don't intrude much."

On the other hand, screenwriter William Goldman remarks, "There are always disagreements. But that's not a bad thing. Bright directors can make tremendous contributions to a script. Basically, the type of picture you have written, along with your own personal attitude and style, will determine the degree of creative participation you have during the shoot."

Traditionally, film is considered the director's medium, television the producer's medium, and theater the writer's medium. All forms require an understanding of their respective relationships and politics.

On the set, each member of the cast and crew want to deliver their best and will offer their opinions. The director must sort all this out and determine priorities. To that end, I suggest that all communication be funneled through the director. As with the rest of the cast and crew—including the art department, camera operators, sound crew, script supervisor, hair and makeup team, props and wardrobe department—close communication, particularly with the director, will ultimately pay off.

Should you have special production requirements such as stunts, special effects or animals, hire a specialist. If you cannot afford to do so, consider omitting the scene. Stunts in films are usually coordinated by a stunt gaffer. Because of potential dangers involved, the DGA offers immediate advice by stunt specialists and it is suggested that story-boards be executed with ample time provided for rehearsals. For the film-ing of hazardous action and fire scenes, always have paramedics standing by. Practically all action scenes should be filmed by multiple cameras.

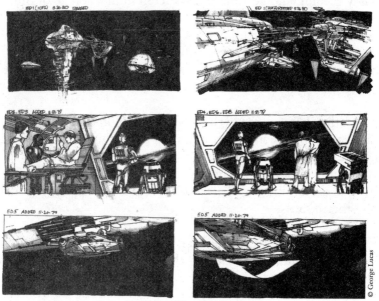

Lucas' Star Wars *Storyboard*

Detailed storyboards are usually provided by the director in order to communicate with the cast and crew involved in a complex and potentially dangerous stunt.

Special effects may be achieved either through special photographic techniques or before the camera when it is actually shooting. The field of computer graphics has been of great use in realizing difficult special effects for film. Today, there are independent groups of special-effects specialists such as George Lucas's Industrial Light and Magic. Effects both generated by computer or created and constructed for live filming are commonly and effectively combined with stunts designed and choreographed by the stunt coordinator.

In regard to film cutting or editing, many directors, for example Hal Ashby and Robert Wise, started as film editors. This can prove beneficial, since the director is deeply involved in the editing process.

Director Stanley Kubrick, among others, has been known to start editing his movies after shooting is completed. It is my opinion that editing should coincide with filming. In most cases, not only is that practical for reshooting and pickup shots, but I believe it is prudent to share this significant function with a creative editor.

The script supervisor should always inform the director if the actor has *mismatched*. For example, in one shot the actor may have lifted a glass of wine to his lips at a specific time and in a certain way. However in the next shot he grasps the glass differently and moves it to his lips at a different dialogue line. This has the potential of creating editing problems, although they are often able to be solved by determining the best place to edit, which could in turn jeopardize the actor's best performance.

It is erroneously perceived that the most outstanding editing occurs in action scenes. I believe that good timing and editorial subtleties are more telling in lyrical or dialogue scenes. Yet, an action-packed movie such as *The French Connection* or *Dances with Wolves* is more likely to garner a best editing award than a comedic drama like *Annie Hall*.

The Motion Picture Association of America (MPAA), instituted a rating system to advise the public about the content of films and to prevent minors from seeing certain films. There is no doubt that American movies are freer today of censorship than ever before. My attitude toward film ratings and censorship is generally liberal. But I believe that films which are excessively violent as well as those that are offensive should be identified and rated as such.

Finally, once you have found a team which works well together as both a technical and creative unit, try to keep this team from film to film.

Many highly regarded directors have worked with the same key crew throughout their careers. Besides helping to ensure the smooth operation of each project, such a procedure helps bring a seamless quality to a long and varied body of work. Hitchcock's films were most often photographed by Gil Taylor with music written by Bernard Hermann. This team, along with others, was available for many of Hitchcock's movies, helping to maintain his signature presence. John Ford, despite arbitrary orders from above during the long years of the Hollywood studio system, remained deeply committed to his crew, and in turn inspired the same loyalty from them. And Woody Allen has used the same tight-knit crew for each of his productions through the years.

LOCATION

Where does the director choose to film the movie? A sound stage, on location, or both? Many factors come into play in order to make that decision. Aesthetic and economic values must be considered.

It is widely known that Hollywood, or more generally Southern California, is firmly established as the world film capital. Not only is the weather consistently temperate throughout the year, but diverse topography ranging from desert to tropics, mountains to sea, as well as cities, suburbs, and farmlands are available within a few hours' drive of Los Angeles.

It should be noted that the International Alliance of Theatrical Stage Employees (IATSE), permits its members to travel thirty miles from L.A. on a per day basis before the production company is obliged to pay for travel, food, and overnight lodging, which would affect the budget negatively.

Among the attractions that certain locations have both to movie actors and producers is the opportunity to exploit a locale because of the prospect of being away. I have even heard of location picks made because of the liking for the native food.

Since the turn of the century, the Hollywood film industry has developed enormously and now contains all the elements and technicians necessary for film production. The most abundant studio space, film laboratories, sound, and postproduction facilities in the world are located in the Los Angeles area. Although this position is constantly being challenged, Hollywood remains the filmmaking hub.

A wide variety of talented film professionals in all specialties, such as directing, writing, producing, animating, music, dance, and graphics, are to be found in Southern California.

In addition, New York—already a major filmmaking locale—Florida, Illinois, North Carolina, Georgia, Texas, parts of Canada and South America, as well as countries in Europe, are all expanding rapidly as production centers.

To inquire about productions currently filming in the United States and to obtain information regarding locations and crew, one may contact state film commissions throughout the country. In addition to taking still shots of a proposed location for the director, the location manager or scout is responsible for obtaining shooting permits. All cities have different shooting ordinances, but most enjoy the notoriety and potential business benefits that filming provides.

Although many directors and actors prefer to shoot on actual or real locations as called for in the story, technology has rapidly advanced whereby computers can now blend location backgrounds with the actor's images filmed on a sound stage. Historically, exteriors were built on studio back lots and matte paintings were extensively used to create location reality. However, this has been supplanted by the computer arts. Despite computer processing, however, there is nothing like the atmosphere of real locations.

Scouting and selecting locations for filming are accomplished by professional location scouts who evaluate several possibilities before recommending specific locales to the director. Final decisions with respect to this are made in consultation with the producer, UPM, production designer, and location manager. If feasible, it is prudent to have the DP, chief grip, electrical gaffer, and sound mixer accompany the director to the final location.

Many factors come into play when determining a location for filming. Is it aesthetically best? Are location fees and permits more prohibitive for the production than working in controlled studio conditions? Is it convenient to cast and crew? Are sound and picture controls better on location or studio? Is there parking access for production vehicles and is equipment readily transportable to the location? Is there access to video playback or screening facilities?

Finally, consideration must be given to lighting and location sound. Exactly when and how long will the location be utilized? The time of day or night will have a bearing on the necessary lighting equipment. This relates to sound as well. It should be determined whether the filming might be disturbed by aircraft flight patterns or be interrupted by sudden and undesirable traffic or pedestrian noises.

Every state in America has a film commission that will gladly provide useful information. Cities as well as countries throughout the world are also eager to accommodate filmmakers and have similar commissions.

Regarding safety and security, twenty-four-hour protection on expensive hot sets is essential, and the prop master should lock up all key props, weapons, and ammunition. Department heads are responsible for the safekeeping of items in their departments.

Students, like nearly everyone else, enjoy visiting locations during shooting. For obvious reasons, visitors are not usually welcome.

On the other hand, it is feasible for film students to make phone arrangements to spend time observing a functioning professional film supply source, an editing room, a videotape facility, and a film *laboratory*. Valuable knowledge is obtainable, especially if these places deal with all formats.

PRODUCTION PLANNING

It stands to reason that a well-informed crew will work harder to contribute their talents than a crew which is simply required to show up and do a job. An attitude of respect and consideration should be established and maintained throughout all phases of production. Along with helping to create a smoothly running shoot, such an atmosphere will greatly reduce possible problems.

In-depth discussions with the entire cast and key personnel, such as the cinematographer, art director, costume designer, and property master, should establish a direction for the tone of the set and look of the film. It is also of value for the director to survey the sets and locations with key crew members. In this way, each person will have an opportunity to confront any potential problems and make suggestions to improve a scene.

Although we generally associate set construction with interiors and exteriors, a film set may be constructed anywhere, normally made of lightweight and portable materials that give an illusion of real places and buildings. The front of a house might be no more than a single wall propped from behind. Dimensions and spatial arrangements are often different from those in the actual world in order to compensate for the limited area of the set as well as the flat screen image.

Colors are also painted with some distortion or exaggeration in order to give proper densities for black–and–white cinematography or to create the tones and hues desired in color cinematography.

To allow for movement in dolly or boom shots, rooms will often have only three walls and no ceilings. Walls referred to as wild can also be moved to allow shooting in all parts of an area, while parts of a ceiling may be suspended to appear in low-angle shots.

Sets must also be constructed to allow installation and placement of sound and lighting equipment. It is possible to actually extend the set by photographing both the scene and an image projected behind it for a rear projection process.

The set decorator is the person who decorates the set with props, furnishings, ornamentations, and artwork.

An excellent way for a director to organize and communicate his thoughts is by creating a storyboard. Similar to a comic strip, a storyboard is a pictorial representation of each shot planned for the film with additional detailed information regarding camera set-ups, camera movements, color coordination and styles for costumes, as well as information about sets and props.

Movie directors such as George Lucas, Steven Spielberg, Alfred Hitchcock, and Stanley Kubrick almost always utilize diagrams or storyboard their films in planning productions. In fact, Hitchcock went so far as to say that his film was more or less completed once he had finished the storyboard, well before the first day of actual shooting.

Significantly important in production planning is for aspiring directors to learn how to time their scenes, Though the script supervisor uses a stopwatch, it is the responsibility of the director to establish the desired timing of each scene. This is more critical in commercials, but less so in features.

In planning the scene shooting order, economical considerations almost always prevail. Regardless of where scenes may appear in a script, all of those scenes are filmed and completed at one time at the sound stage or location.

Special consideration is also given to principal cast scheduling. This is determined in what as known as a *day-out-of-days schedule*. Inasmuch as principal actors are contracted on a weekly basis, they must be paid even though they may not perform.

Working with a realistic, accurate budget and detailed storyboard, while coordinating the details of production planning with a talented, unified, and committed crew, are essential elements to realizing your vision and avoiding disaster.

FILMING TECHNIQUES AND STUNTS

In what format or gauge will the director choose to film—8, 16, or 35 millimeter? Super 16 or 70 millimeter? Color or black and white? Film or videotape?

When planning the film format, careful consideration should be given to opticals and stunts.

The stunt coordinator traditionally supervised the planning and execution of stunts. That job used to be handled by the stuntmen themselves, but since the complexity and dangers have increased over the years, the need for a stunt designer is paramount.

Should your film include stunts, you might want to familiarize yourself with the varied techniques and approaches of some notable stunt designers and action film directors, both past and present. Among the renowned stunt pioneers of the past are Yakimo Canutt, who designed the chariot race in *Ben Hur*. Subsequently, Dar Robinson, stunt coordinator for the car chase in *Bullitt*, and Hal Needham, a former stunt man, became outstanding action directors themselves .

A ten-minute film called *The Great Train Robbery*, made by G.M. Anderson in 1903, gave birth to a plethora of classic American westerns. This remarkably resilient film genre, which has survived with topical variations through the years, is almost always packed with boisterous stunts, from stage coach and train robberies to pursuits on horseback through rugged terrain to barroom brawls.

The twenties brought more than a score of new directors into the western fold, most notably John Ford, Raoul Walsh, James Cruze, and stars such as the exciting Buck Jones, Tim McCoy, and the extremely popular Tom Mix.

After a decade of appearing in low-budget westerns, film icon John Wayne first achieved stardom in John Ford's classic *Stagecoach*, which garnered an Oscar nomination, virtually unheard of for a film in the western genre. Wayne was to be followed by war-hero/western star Audie Murphy. Prominent also as western directors are Fred Zinnemann and George Stevens, in whose films Gary Cooper and Alan Ladd starred.

The gangster film, another action genre involving getaway scenes, gunfire, and so on, roared to prominence in the early 1930s with the help of highly talented actors like Edward G. Robinson and James Cagney. And the *film noir* genre, coming to prominence in the late 1940s and early 1950s with such classic films as Howard Hawks's *The Big Sleep* and Raoul Walsh's *White Heat*, continued to explore the underbelly of society, albeit in a highly stylized, darkly lit manner, providing some additional work for Hollywood stuntmen. In 1967, Arthur Penn gave a new spin to gangsterism with his provocative, violent *Bonnie and Clyde*, starring Warren Beatty and Faye Dunaway. The troubled characters the stars portrayed joined with other gangsters to become legendary American antiheroes.

Maverick Sam Peckinpah, who directed *The Wild Bunch* in 1969 and *The Getaway* in 1972, is especially noted for his artful, even poetic depiction of violence. More recently, some notable filmmakers from abroad are directing prominent action films in America. Europeans Renny Harlin and Paul Verhoeven, respectively, directed such expensive vehicles for action stars Bruce Willis and Arnold Schwarzenegger as *Die Hard 2* and *Total Recall*. The overwhelming popularity of the action film genre in Hong Kong has produced the talented John Woo, who directed Nicholas Cage and John Travolta in the 1997 action-suspense film *Face/Off*, a film which received a great deal of attention for the lyrical, balletic, often breathtaking scope of its complex action scenes. Like Peckinpah, he too employs slow motion to sometimes eerie effect.

Once in a great while an otherwise mediocre film is made memorable for a particularly good stunt sequence. For example, *They Live*, John Carpenter's 1988 sci-fi satire, contains a remarkable, completely engaging 7 1/2 minute wordless, unscored fist fight sequence which was rehearsed for four weeks and took four days to shoot. This proves that big-budget explosions are not necessary to capture the attention of today's jaded action audience.

Whatever your stance on violence, it is academic that conflict is the motivation for plot. Raymond Chandler, whose mystery stories have been successfully adapted to screen as film noir, stated, "When in doubt, have two guys come through the door with guns."

directing fight scene with stunt man

Today more than ever, stunts have become the true stars of certain types of big-budget action films, often overshadowing such essentials as story line and character development. While filming stunts, tragedies have inevitably occurred and even more often have been narrowly avoided. To complicate matters, some high-profile stars, such as Tom Cruise, insist on doing many of their own hazardous stunts.

Regardless of the genre, I feel strongly that all stunts should be planned and supervised by the director. This is not only essential creatively, but is absolutely crucial for safety. Safety during shooting is clearly the ultimate responsibility of the director. I have come to the conclusion that the director is most qualified to supervise the shooting

37

of action sequences, primarily because he is usually not intent on film-ing stunts in one breathtaking shot. Directors tend to break up shots for maximum effect. Useful stunt safety information is available from the Stunt International Association or the Stunt Women's Association.

All firearms used by students in my film classes are made of plastic, and knives are made of rubber. The use of actual firearms as props, as well as the actual consumption of alcohol, is for obvious reasons strictly forbidden. I do permit student actors to smoke in scenes if they wish. I also heartily encourage the use of fake blood, as well as the use of oral blood capsules, to add a sense of reality.

Action scenes are staged so that the camera operator makes sure that space between principals is not visible at the point of simulated contact. In postproduction, the sound effects editor will add or accentuate the sounds of a hit, blow, crashing chair, broken glass, and so on as required, as well as extraneous sounds to help create maximum verisimilitude.

During filming professional movies, all firearms are under the supervision of the *armorer* at all times. Blank shells, or squibs, used to resemble a ricochet, are potentially dangerous and are under the supervision of the special effects department. Now, "dust guns" are commonly used because they are faster and easier to set up. Though available in half and full load blank shells, mostly quarter load blanks are used. Gunfire sound effects are added in postproduction.

Having directed numerous television episodes involving fire, I am well accustomed to filming blazes. That too requires special knowledge and preparation, the least of which necessitates providing standby firemen and proper protective fire gear for cast and crew.

Not only does movie paraphernalia have a fascination and value to souvenir-hunters, but tourists and collectors seem to cherish movie mementos. More than once I have had production delayed because valuable items from the set were missing. Another annoying hindrance to production has to do with tabloid photographers and videographers sneaking onto closed sets with phony passes, who must then be removed upon detection while production stops. Such events may distract both talent and crew, especially during preparation for or shooting of a complex action sequence, when such distraction can turn dangerous. It is vital to keep tight security both on set and on location, especially when dealing with well-known actors, when such problems are most likely to crop up.

It is extremely important, considering the stress, long hours and rigors of shooting, to emphasize the importance of maintaining good physical conditioning by directors. Concerning relaxing during shooting, director Sidney Lumet said, "No matter how pressured it gets, I learned in the Army how to nap wherever I was."

As for useful equipment during the shoot, directors now may utilize an ingenious film and video camera stabilizing device called the *Steadicam*, devised by Garrett Brown, that enables the camera operator to keep the camera steady off the tripod during action as well as handheld shots. This innovation, used effectively in the filming of *Rocky*, for example, has brought a new freedom to directors and has affected the look of many contemporary films.

As for dailies, some directors prefer to view dailies transferred to videocassette in privacy, while others elect to study rushes on a large screen, comparable to that of a commercial theater. In my opinion, as long as the screening of dailies are held discretely, they could be helpful to the director, editors, key crew personnel, and interested actors.

Instant video playback can also be a great advantage to director, crew, and cast, because returning to locations is usually impractical and costly.

Actor Jerry Lewis insisted on using this technique back in 1949 during his first movie, *My Friend Irma*, at Paramount Pictures.

For those shooting in Los Angeles, it is immeasurably useful to have a production directory which includes information on where to rent everything from props and trucks to addresses of film processors and casting facilities. In Los Angeles, two such directories are *The Hollywood Reporter Blue Book* and *LA 411*. Such highly useful regional directories, published annually, are available in most cities with a high volume of production activity. For example, when planning a shoot in New York City you might use the *New York Production Guide*.

Will the picture be optically blown-up, or enlarged from 16mm to conventional 35 millimeter? Will the sound be recorded in *Dolby*? The selection of camera equipment is usually the responsibility of the DP. Often the choice of lenses is mutually decided upon by both the director and DP. But many hands-on directors, such as Sidney Lumet, John Frankenheimer, and Stanley Kubrick, determine the lens for each shot.

There are four primary elements that affect the picture produced in the camera. First, there is the light that exists before the image enters the lens. Second, there are color filters and nets or light diffusers. Third, there is the size of the lens itself. Fourth is the lens aperture or opening which determines the amount of light that will pass through the lens onto the film. Other factors also come into play, such as the angle of the shutter and the negative stock.

The most fundamental photographic choice the DP and director make is the specific lens to be used for a particular shot.

Technically, we refer to lenses on the lower millimeter range such as 9mm, 14mm, 17mm, 18mm, and 21mm, as wide–angle lenses. Those ranging from 75mm up are referred to as long lenses.

BLOCKING AND STAGING

When rehearsing, I have found the most effective way to block and stage a scene is to have the actors, writer, AD, DP, and script supervisor present.

First, we read the scene, interpreting and making suggestions all the while, which frequently results in dialogue changes. The technique of reading while sitting around a table was born in the theater and is now used in both movies and television. By doing this, major dialogue changes may be worked out, thus avoiding problems during production.

I believe that giving the actors freedom is most important, and that means the director sitting back and observing where actors take the scene and at what tempo. Are the actors' lines and moves believable? Do not be dictatorial. Suggest and accommodate. Then, set the camera angle.

While observing John Huston direct Albert Finney in *Annie*, I noticed the director asked if Mr. Finney would feel more comfortable by slightly adjusting his position. Many problems are solved by such simple acts of courtesy.

On the other hand, Alfred Hitchcock, who meticulously preblocked his scenes, expected his actors to follow his precise directives. Hitchcock would, however, sometimes reshoot a scene on the spur of the moment, changing one small detail, like the removal of a coat, to very slightly alter style or mood. He would then make his final choice during editing.

In general, I would suggest that you encourage improvisation and the free flow of ideas. But be prepared to make your points and win your skirmishes with sound argument and focused, concise articulation. Michael Curtiz, the Hungarian-born director of *Casablanca*, known for his emotional outbursts on set, would provide a useless directive to a western actor, saying, "Just ride off in all directions. . ." Then, Curtiz would complain to his assistant, "Next time I send an idiot, I'll go myself!"

Always consult your director of photography regarding blocking and staging; he or she will likely have a different perception about how to proceed. Such new visions can be helpful and should be thoroughly welcomed.

Probably the most common question regarding blocking and staging asked by aspiring filmmakers is, "How can I avoid crossing the line?"

The simple reply is that you cannot always avoid it. Some fine filmmakers, notably Jean-Luc Godard, have pointedly and consistently crossed the line without harming their movie's dramatic effect. But if you do experiment, you must have a consistent inner vision; that is, you must know what you are doing.

In *Psycho*, director Alfred Hitchcock, who had been a film editor, exited a character from right to left, then had the same character suddenly reenter the same scene from right to left. Though technically unorthodox, the knowledgeable director managed to scare the hell out of the audience by using this unconventional device.

Generally, it is important to keep the viewer oriented, and that is accomplished by maintaining consistent camera angles, such as left to right and right to left. Bear in mind that one must understand the rules before breaking them.

My feeling is that although storyboarding a sequence helps the director communicate with cast and crew for intricate and complex shooting, I do not recommend its use for regular sequences. Too many variables occur and I prefer not to be rigid about shot design. However when transmitting a rather detailed image to the crew, especially when shooting a stunt, fantasy, or science-fiction film, storyboarding is most often an essential tool of effective, precise communication.

A shot is not merely a picture nor is it a still photograph. The film shot is part of a montage. Consequently, the angle with which a shot is chosen will contribute to the meaning of the montage.

Any subsequent change from a normal point of view ought to be used to support the director's intended meaning. For example, a proud or overbearing character could be filmed from a low angle, the fore-shortened perspective stressing these traits. Conversely, an oppressed or dispirited individual could be shot from a high angle. Horror and suspense films sometimes make rather free use of highly unusual camera angles to convey an air of the unnatural or of menace.

After the blocking and staging is set, stand-ins are used by the DP and lighting team while the principals are off preparing their wardrobe, hair and makeup, thereby giving the DP time to complete the lighting. This is also a valuable time for the director to communicate with actors and crew.

While treating the subjects of blocking and staging in the classroom, I screen a diverse selection of films for my students. First, I present a synopsis of the stories. Then, stopping at various scenes, I help them analyze the staging as well as other salient aspects of direction and production.

I screen Elia Kazan's *East of Eden* to study his ability to elicit acutely felt, highly credible performances in scenes of great power, with directing choices that helped allow the talented James Dean, Julie Harris, Raymond Massey, Jo Van Fleet, and others to do some of their best work. Another film we analyze in class is *Lawrence of Arabia*.

We focus on former film editor David Lean's epic by paying special attention to the dramatic juxtaposition of sweeping landscape and intimate character study. For me, *The Four Hundred Blows*, by Francois Truffaut, is especially useful to study in class because of its break with traditional filmmaking techniques, as it incorporates a fresh style that meshes particularly well with its unconventional, autobiographical treatment of wayward youth. Finally we study *Paper Moon*, by director Peter Bogdanovich. This American period comedy pays homage to directors such as Preston Sturgis and Billy Wilder, and follows the misadventures of a con man father and his little girl. We analyze how blocking and staging choices help promote a sense of intimacy with these two dynamic characters, propel the plot forward, or accentuate a comic moment.

If time permits, I screen my own early works in class, paying close attention to choices of blocking and staging, enabling filmmaking students to see what I was attempting to do at their time of life with various scenes.

We also discuss the birth of television and its unforeseen effects on the film industry. The 1950s were a period of significant changes in movies. Facing the challenge of television, the motion picture industry fought back with some gimmicks of its own, such as 3-D, CinemaScope, and other screen processes. The proliferation of independent productions propelled the erosion of the old studio-factory system with its stables of contract artists and its systematic star building. The very cost of the star-building system now became prohibitive. Two of the stars promoted in the classic Hollywood manner were Marilyn Monroe and James Dean, and their early deaths seemed to symbolize the end of an era.

Regarding the old studio system, although it provided career security to rising stars and directors, it severely limited their artistic choices. Many quaked at the sound of authority issuing from studio heads such as Samuel Goldwyn, although much of what he said is quotable nonsense, such as his forceful, "Include me out!" or his response to a director's plea, "I can answer you in just two words: Im--possible."

The new procedure, involving more and more independent producers releasing their movies through the old studios, put more power in the hands of directors, and breathed new life into the film industry. Television, the supposed menace, also was to prove productive in terms of new ideas, which fed into the making of movies for theatrical release. Some of these were spin-offs from television programs such as the group of films based on Paddy Chayefsky's teleplays, including "Marty" and "Bachelor Party." Ironically, Chayevsky later went on to write the most scathing indictment of television culture in Sidney Lumet's *Network*.

Interesting and significant was the proportion of directors who served their apprenticeship in television. People such as Arthur Penn, John Frankenheimer, Sidney Lumet, Robert Mulligan, Delbert Mann, and numerous others went on to successful careers as film directors.

In any event, whether directing for small screen or cinema, whether making an action flick or a small independent feature, you must prepare your talent so they may do their best work. Some directors rant, some of them are gentle, some of them are vague. But they all must communicate. The director must know what his actors want to do, and he must also be true to himself while understanding how other people behave. He must understand the craft.

On a more prosaic level, we turn to actor Spencer Tracy, who, when rehearsing a scene with a nervous young actor, advised, "Just learn your lines and don't bump into the furniture."

DIRECTING SHORTS, COMMERCIALS, AND MUSIC VIDEOS

Almost all filming formats are employed, such as videotape, 16mm or 35mm film, and approaches vary for each director.

Essentially, in directing features, it is my belief that the director must have a strong sense of narrative writing which unfolds in approximately ninety minutes.

With television commercials, it is the director's job to convey the commercial message in increments of fifteen, thirty, or sixty seconds. Often, specific scenes from the sixty-second commercial are lifted and used to form shorter-length commercials. Directorial focus is always on selling products, but one may use drama, comedy, and other devices to communicate with the mass audience.

For me, the most interesting aspect in making today's commercials is the use of casting, which emphasizes real voices and ordinary people, as exemplified by directors Joe Sedelmaier and Joe Pytka. Sedelmaier says, "I do all of my casting in the Midwest because it's the only place where I can find average–looking people." Pytka is perhaps best known for his McDonald's ad starring basketball legends Michael Jordan and Larry Byrd.

Pytka, like noted directors Adrian Lyne and Richard Lester, have been known to alternate between commercials and features, making up to $15,000 a day, plus costs. Ridley Scott, who worked for years as set designer and director of hundreds of television commercials, went on to direct *The Duellists*, *Alien*, and *Thelma & Louise*.

While directing commercials can be a good gateway to film directing, important differences exist between feature film and commercial directing. Obviously, in commercials, script and storyboard are usually created by an advertising agency copywriter and art director. But the discipline and precision required of a director of commercials are certainly good habits to cultivate.

Inasmuch as my own beginnings are in making both commercials and short films, I encourage students to take a similar direction, advising them to shoot their short films on videotape.

When I was in my twenties, I made my first short film, *The Shoes*, in 35mm, which was a mistake. I subsequently learned that 16mm, at one third the cost, would have been equally effective when blown up to a 35mm format in a laboratory.

Some filmmakers, in an effort to cut production costs, often use *short-ends*. Short-ends are the unused portion of the raw stock film that is removed from the magazine, then recanned for possible future use, or sale to raw stock outlets. Although somewhat inconvenient, using short-ends of raw stock will constitute considerable savings.

Finally, I suggest that students enter their short films in as many international competitions as possible, with the idea of using them as a lever to acquiring a distributor or directing assignment from a producer.

I am amazed at how many students make a beeline toward me to express their passion for music videos.

One enthusiast, Drew Stone, said, "Being a singer with a hardcore band called Antidote, as well as a movie fan, led to the opportunity to direct my first music video for our band. Then, a rap group called Onyx saw the little film I made, liked it and asked me to produce a music video for them."

Inasmuch as most students have enrolled in my classes to learn how to direct features, I discourage them from concentrating on music videos and urge them to concentrate on aspects of narrative full-length features. Promoting the marketability of a pop star and his latest musical release is hardly my idea of learning how to direct feature-length movies. However, music videos are part of our culture today.

Like regular commercials, music videos must convey a strong image or message in a very short time span. Unlike regular commercials, however, music videos very often leave the director rather free to extrapolate from whatever images a particular song brings to mind, as the point is to create a mood rather than convey a bit of precise information about a product. The director often enjoys a great deal of leeway in technique and sometimes even choice of actual subject matter, which need not always correspond exactly to that of the song's lyrics. You get to create a series of images more or less from scratch, as it were. However, the videos that are most interesting to me personally possess contrapuntal images that accompany the songs' lyrics. One strong plus for those students who are interested in this field is the constant proliferation of unsigned bands needing promotion. This situation of course creates a void which even novices might fill to practice their craft. If one of the local bands you work with actually gets a contract, your work may receive notice too.

Among the most successful music video directors are David Fincher, Dominic Sena, and Spike Jonze.

The most practical advice I can give to aspiring music video directors is to concentrate on studying music and graphics, then try getting an apprenticeship or job with a music video production company. Sometimes, thriving pop groups with their own funding will hire a director they especially like and produce their own music videos.

MUSIC

The film medium has traditionally offered vast opportunities for composers, although a recent, successful trend toward cross–marketing films with CDs has created a tendency for directors to choose established hit songs of a particular period over original music. This has the advantage of immediately setting a film's mood, producing a heavily promoted, briskly selling compilation record, and scratching off the film scorer's name from the budget sheet all at the same time.

In the days of silent filmmaking, the choice of film music was an especially vital one. Some early directors, such as Charlie Chaplin, wrote their own scores, for example, the melodious and plaintiff music for *City Lights*. The great classical composer Sergei Prokofiev was engaged by director Sergei Eisenstein to write the film score for *Battleship Potemkin*, and their collaboration is one of the great stories of director-composer accord. In fact, Eisenstein would marvel at how Prokofiev could view a scene, then come back with music that matched its tone and pacing exactly. The works of classical composers have been freely used in a great variety of films, from period dramas to New Wave cinema to Disney features to slapstick comedy.

Countless talented composers have turned to scoring and found it to be fulfilling. Tiomkin, one of the most prolific composers in Hollywood, upon winning an Academy Award for scoring *The High and the Mighty*, quipped, "I would like to thank my colleagues, Brahms, Bach, Beethoven, Richard Strauss. . ."

Until his death in 1970, the versatile Alfred Newman supervised and conducted the famous Twentieth Century Fox orchestra. Newman's nephew, Randy, a successful pop composer and performer, followed in the family's footsteps and wrote the musical scores for *Ragtime*, *The Natural*, and *Parenthood*.

51

Another composer of especial note is Nino Rota, whose disarming motifs appeared in the great works of Fellini as well as others. Bernard Hermann, whose haunting melodies and series of unresolved chords and arpeggios helped create the unsettling, compulsive tone to many Hitchcock films, is probably best known for composing the musical motif of Hitchcock's thriller *Psycho*. Among other renowned movie composers are Aaron Copland, Max Steiner, Ernest Gold, Jerry Goldsmith, John Barry, Michel Legrand, John Williams, and Lalo Shifrin.

Generally, it is neither necessary nor desirable to use music throughout an entire film. An improper choice of music may easily detract from a film. Film music should be used for purposeful effect, to introduce, guide, punctuate, enlighten, and set the tone. Composer Elmer Bernstein said, "I'm often asked by movie directors to score a sequence simply to keep it lively."

Location music is simply the music which is recorded on location at an event, then later used on the sound track. A music documentary film such as *Woodstock* is a good example of the use of live music.

Original scored music is obviously more problematic, as many choices are involved in incorporating original music successfully into your film. It is important that you carefully choose your film scorer because there are many skillful composers who simply cannot write for film. Most skilled film scorers are able to write well in a variety of styles.

Composers must possess an unusual measure of self–discipline because the complex motif that they wish to develop runs for twenty minutes, but may only be required for sixty seconds. It can prove trying to discover someone who is both musically gifted and who possesses other, more difficult-to-measure qualities as well. A fine film composer can add immeasurably to a film. Consider Bernard Hermann's comment on composing for film: "I feel that music on the screen can reveal the inner thoughts of the characters."

When choosing a composer for your film, you must be aware of your music budget. You will need to add up the union rate for the composer, as well as rates for musicians, copying fees, recording fees, arranging, transfer of original tape to larger magnetic tape for cutting and mixing, studio time as well as any additional fees negotiated for the composer.

In certain situations, an existing musical composition is rerecorded for use in a film and permission is required from the publisher. By rerecording, alterations can be made which usually enhance the fidelity and change the timing.

Timing is an integral part of scoring for film. In animation, some music may be written and prerecorded to a storyboard, necessitating the picture to be executed to the track.

Most live–action filmmaking requires music to be composed during postproduction after the film has been edited. The composer works to footage with thirty feet in 16mm film equaling one minute. Minutes may further be tallied into fifteen feet for thirty seconds, and so forth. In smaller increments, the composer figures the standard twenty-four frames per second, twelve frames per half second, and six frames for a quarter second. In 35mm, ninety feet represents one minute while frame counts remain the same.

At the recording session, a *click track*, which functions as a kind of metronome, is provided through headsets. If, for example, the music needs a beat at each twelve frames in order to cut to the film, the sound of a click will be heard every half second. After the music is recorded and matched with the film, the picture and track are synchronized.

Your third choice as director when choosing music for your film is to make use of the abundant supply of library scores. In fact, most film music is selected from these sources. There are about twenty-thousand selections available from professional film music libraries.

A creative music editor is sensitive to pacing and mood and may successfully score a film even if he is not a professional musician or composer. The director often helps choose the music to be used. Then, the film editor must cut and splice the film until music and image work as a whole. Since the accents in the music will come at arbitrary points, the music editor usually selects the most important visual action and lines up an accent in the music with that action in the picture. He then runs the piece back and listens to the entire scene from the beginning. Many such trial and error placements will be required before a suitable film to music marriage is made, with music cutting, lengthening, or cross–fading to another composition all possible options.

Another possibility to keep in mind as director is to choose key scenes and pick music for them before editing, so that the film itself may be edited to the rhythms of the score. To suit the needs of an offbeat film, an innovative filmmaker may come up with an entirely new plan. For example, it is possible for the filmmaker to compose his own music, or something like music, by making marks directly on the sound track of the celluloid film.

In any event, a gifted music editor can provide an excellent score from library music, using a process which is usually far less expensive than hiring a composer to provide original music. Therefore, when working under tight budgetary constraints, using a diverse music library is wise, especially if you can find a music editor who has a special feel for this work.

POSTPRODUCTION

In the Golden Age of movies, directors rarely edited their pictures, leaving instead the chores of postproduction to producers. Editors were referred to as cutters, not editors, because the editorial decisions remained in the hands of the producer.

Lillian Roth, in her book *Picture* records letters between John Huston and Dore Schary, then studio head at MGM. "Dear John," the chief executive wrote, "I don't know if you have seen the finished print of *The Red Badge of Courage*, but we had to make some cuts that were essential. I don't believe that we sacrificed any of the integrity you poured into this movie and hope you like what we have accomplished. Fondly, Dore." The very thought of receiving such a frank, cheerful memo today would send many directors into fits.

It wasn't until more recently that directors such as George Lucas, Steven Spielberg, and Francis Ford Coppola started the trend of filmmakers getting deeply involved with editing, sound, music, and all phases of postproduction, including marketing.

The director's cut in both movies and television is defined by the DGA contract and is usually considered an important bargaining point. But the final cut is still usually reserved by producers and major film companies, who cite pressures concerning scheduling, marketing, ratings, and censorship. Directors who have achieved enormous box office success may have enough power to demand final cut. If there is strong disagreement on the matter, the controversy at times becomes public, with an angry director separately releasing his own version of the completed film, either in the theater or on videotape.

Certainly, the power of the editing process is enormous. A bad edit can literally butcher a film, cutting it to shreds, so to speak. Conversely, a hopelessly flawed shoot can sometimes be transformed into a filmic swan by a skilled editor. The wisest directors encourage editors to make the first cut and keep open the idea of optical effects. Hopefully you have chosen an editor during preproduction whose style and approach are compatible with your own, for the integrity of your film depends on a good edit. Editing involves more than merely cutting and splicing film, requiring sophisticated technical, artistic, and dramatic skills to produce a coherent finished product that is at the same time totally compatible with the director's vision and intent. The best directors of today almost always have an extremely fine relationship with their editors, choosing the same editors for each of their films, and working closely with them to achieve the finished product.

Often during preproduction, editors and directors plan much of the editing. Then, during shooting, the editor may confer with the director about the previous day's rushes and tentatively begin to assemble parts of the film. After shooting is complete, the editor will work with this material to make a rough cut in sync with the sound tracks, and this constitutes the first work print. Other directors and editors might agree to begin the editing process only after filming is complete. Still others opt to explore much more unorthodox methods, such as making great use of improvisation during filming, then putting together a variety of rough cuts, each promoting different moods or styles.

As a final aside, it is interesting to note that in the very beginning of filmmaking history, there were no film editors, for entire films were made from one take or shot from an immobile camera. After a few years, people began to explore the idea that perhaps one could cut and splice the film without disorienting the audience. In 1903, it was Edwin Porter who made filmmaking history with both *The Life of an American Fireman* and *The Great Train Robbery* for the Edison

Company. Both films used simple cross-cutting techniques. Shortly thereafter, D.W. Griffith introduced all of the basic concepts of film editing we use today. Notably, Sergei Eisenstein in Russia and G.W. Pabst in Germany refined and expanded the craft of editing, working with the concepts of montage and invisible cutting, respectively.

As for sound editing, I find it interesting that geography and movie history have affected the significance of on-camera sound as well as the aesthetics and business of films. Even renowned filmmakers such as Federico Fellini, Michelangelo Antonioni, Francois Truffaut, and Akira Kurosawa have all blithely filmed without concerns about location, sound, or dialogue, improvising dialogue later in dubbing, primarily because it was more expedient and economical. Hollywood developed a different perception, especially as America could count on most of the world audience. And the American audience has never gotten used to either substandard audio quality or the very idea of a dubbed film; most find it unbearably annoying to watch lips move in discordance with sound, while the rest of the world regards us, perhaps enviously, as somewhat spoiled by our demand for technical precision. Those Americans who will sit still for a foreign film usually prefer subtitles. In any event, it was in the United States that on-camera sound was perfected as we know it.

The film is prepared for the composer and sound effects editor by *spotting* it. This process determines precisely where music and effects will be placed in relation to the images. The sound editor generally will assemble and synchronize both special effects and music tracks. It is the role of the film editor to work with the dialogue and voice-over.

Colors and tints may be altered after consultation among the director, cinematographer, and laboratory technician by what is known as *timing*. This printing process is generally performed with the aim of achieved desired consistency of density and color values within the scenes of the film.

Rerecording, sometimes referred to as mixing, is one of the final processes before a film's release, and involves mixing several sound tracks onto one final track. Finally, *negative cutting*, or conforming, is the final conformation of picture and negative in the laboratory. The negative is edited so that it matches the final work print of the film. Dupe negatives are derived from a master print of the original negative, and are made both to produce your release prints and protect the originally cut negative.

Your film is almost ready for release. Title, screen credits, advertising and promotion, though traditionally neglected by filmmakers, should be of great interest for they help present your film to the world. The typography of the title, usually similar in all media, is an important detail. There have been many outstanding graphic designers, but the classic works of Saul Bass, who conceived and animated the main title for *Man with the Golden Arm*; Maurice Binder, who designed numerous James Bond movie titles; and Pablo Ferro, who designed and executed the titles for *Dr. Strangelove*, are exemplary. Now, with computer generated art and the influences of music video graphics, Nina Saxon, designer of *Forrest Gump*, and Kyle Cooper, designer of *Seven*, have become significant names in film titling.

As for credits, the DGA stipulates that if the director's name precedes all other film credits, it must also appear as the last credit on all media advertising. Regarding titles and screen copyrights, I find it interesting and amusing that film and television distributors, usually responsible for obtaining copyright notices, have traditionally indicated the distribution date by Roman numerals. This somewhat masks the original distribution date, so that audiences may not be aware they are watching an older film.

Depictions of movie stars in posters and billboards has always had great impact, and the rarer specimens of yesteryear sometimes fetch many thousands of dollars at auction. If you are lucky enough to have a marketing campaign at work for your film, you should try to have as much input as possible into its thrust. Many a good film has been stopped dead in its tracks by a marketing approach that for some reason or another failed to communicate the film's special strengths.

Tie-ins for movie advertising have become a gigantic business with corporations such as General Mills, Ford, and McDonald's seeking maximum product and logo exposure. Converting characters, cars, and costumes from a film into toys or novelty items is also a popular way to generate and maintain both interest and additional revenues. This is traditionally accomplished by licensing third parties who manufacture and sell these products. It is of note that

George Lucas actually had marketing in mind before creating the unique characters and vehicles for *Star Wars*.

Star Wars

Other advertising tools such as preview screenings and documentaries depicting the making of a movie are also ways to help generate that all-important "buzz."

PREPARING A SAMPLE REEL

In preparing a sample of your directing work, avoid using clips or short sequences, providing instead a substantial scene not exceeding ten minutes in length. Busy employers, agents, and producers simply do not have the time to view anything much longer. Ideally, these people would like to pop something into their videocassette player for a quick look. Should they be interested, further communication will likely ensue.

I therefore recommend that you present your sample reel in VHS 1/2" color videotape. At this stage, don't worry about picture definition and clarity. Prospective employers and producers are mostly concerned with how a potential director handles story material, actors, blocking, and editing, and how production-efficient he or she is.

Employers are usually bombarded by slick-looking promotional material, so try to avoid the barrage by simply creating a professional-looking sample of your work.

Because of time constraints, it might be wise to even eliminate the customary long academy leader preceding your videotape. Mainly, keep your sample reel simple. And always keep your reel ready to screen. You might get a call to make it available immediately.

PITCHING

When teaching, I give one written assignment, which entails writing a two– or three–page sales or "pitch" letter to a real source for film funding,.

Regarding budget, my advice to aspiring film directors is to keep it well under $1,000,000.

Regarding verbal pitches, which can be most effective, I sight the pitches as depicted in director Robert Altman's movie *The Player* and the meetings that actor Kevin Bacon had as a fledgling director in *The Big Picture*. In both stories, I note the tendency by busy executives to generalize and categorize both ideas and talents. Try to be concise and express a willingness to listen and cooperate.

During the last couple of decades, the term *high concept* has crept into the show business lexicon. The phrase was originally used to describe certain easily grasped material, often expressed as punchy blurbs for television. For example, "Man accused of murdering wife is pursued by police."

High concept ideas are usually difficult to sell to studios or producers because that genre is often originated by the studios or producers themselves, although it is true that succinct pitching helps aspiring directors present their projects in a clear way.

AGENTS AND DIRECTING ASSIGNMENTS

They are not easy to come by.

After lots of study and hard work, obtaining an agent and getting a directing assignment is a major chore. A good place to start is the DGA directory that contains an index of accredited agents. Agencies that represent new directors usually assign someone to deal expressly with newcomers. Once accepted, your sample reel is evaluated in order to select the material that warrants closer scrutiny.

I believe it is most effective to write a brief letter adressesed to the person within the agency in charge of seeking and representing new directing talent. Do not try to communicate with the principals. Follow up. Remember, before pursuing this, have your reel ready.

In order to keep abreast of the frequent personnel changes as well as current production activity, it is essential that you read the trade publications, namely, *Daily Variety*, *The Hollywood Reporter*, and *Weekly Variety*.

Though difficult, it is possible to acquire a directing assignment without an agent. When a student does get the opportunity to pitch to an agent, not only must he or she be confident, but must know the material in question thoroughly. For example, in episodic television, a potential employer can quickly determine if an aspiring director really knows the show and its characters and is not merely pitching for a job while waiting for the opportunity to direct a big feature.

Sue Mengers, agent for renowned film directors and movie stars, when asked what she looked for when taking on a client, said, "Money.

The potential to earn money. I'm really not interested in signing up new clients unless any of my regulars leave me."

Regarding the packaging of first-time directors, Mengers remarked, "The key in their case is good material for the lowest possible budget."

Movie director Charles Matthau, who aspired to make a larger budgeted film after his first feature, says, "They will increase your budget only if your preceding film makes a lot of money."

Finally, I believe it is advantageous to become a member of the Directors Guild of America. Call the DGA for information on obtaining membership. Usually very accommodating, the Guild provides special consideration for women and ethnic minorities.

Moving up through the ranks to become a sought-after director is a long and difficult process. Although not everyone who joins the Guild becomes a working director, he or she can still enjoy the benefits of Guild membership.

In order to become a UPM, a first AD, or a second AD, applicants must have obtained employment with a company that has signed a collective bargaining agreement with the Directors Guild of America.

MINORITY FILM DIRECTORS

At first, women, African Americans, Latinos, and Asians had difficulty breaking into the U.S. entertainment industry.

In the 1930s, Hollywood began to woo successful playwrights. A number of these happened to be women such as Dorothy Parker, Lillian Hellman, and Anita Loos, who began writing screenplays. Claire Booth Luce, noted as a playwright, also created stories for films.

Only since the late thirties and forties did women such as Leni Riefenstahl, Ida Lupino, and Dorothy Arzner get the opportunity to direct movies. More recently, many more women have joined the ranks. Enjoying notable success are Martha Coolidge, Amy Heckerling, Barbra Streisand, Penny Marshall, Jane Campion, Kasi Lemmons and Nora Ephron, among others. Ephron directed *Sleepless in Seattle* before going on to direct the enchanting feature *Michael*.

As executives and producers, Sherry Lansing, Marcy Carsey, and Lynda Obst are most prominent. Recently, Obst observed, "Since I have been in Hollywood, the movie business has undergone systemic transformation and personality changes as well as turnarounds in attitude regarding opportunities for both gender and race."

Regarding African Americans, it wasn't until the 1960s that directors Spike Lee, Gordon Parks, Sidney Poitier, and Melvin Van Peebles, rose to prominence. More recently, Robert Townsend, John Singleton, Mario Van Peebles, and Kasi Lemmons have joined their ranks. The talented Ms. Lemmons's first feature, *Eve's Bayou*, for which she also wrote the original screenplay, received an unusual degree of both critical and commercial acclaim for a novice director.

Among the notable American Latino movie directors are Edward James Olmos and Robert Rodriguez. While still at the University of Texas, Rodriguez shot his first feature, entitled *El Mariachi*, as an extra-curricular project in two weeks for just $7,000. The film made big waves and Mr. Rodriguez wound up with a multipicture deal. Since then, his experience has become an inspiration to aspiring film directors everywhere.

Wayne Wang and Gregg Araki are most noteworthy among Asian-American directors. Among Wang's films are *The Joy Luck Club* and *Smoke*. Araki, whose troubling, provocative films make him the spokesman for today's disaffected youth, has directed *The Doom Generation* and *Nowhere*, which have already achieved cult status. And the prominent John Woo, who hails from Hong Kong but of late has carved a niche in big-budget American moviemaking, has directed *Broken Arrow* and *Face/Off*, among others.

It is interesting to note that many of the above–mentioned directors started as either writers or actors.

CONTEMPORARY FILMMAKERS

When one thinks of talented contemporary directors, two that immediately come to mind are Steven Spielberg and Francis Ford Coppola, but of course there are numerous other fine filmmakers.

Those whose work I have found most consistently interesting are Woody Allen, Bernardo Bertolucci, Albert Brooks, Mel Brooks, Tim Burton, Jane Campion, John Cassavetes, Joel and Ethan Coen, Clint Eastwood, Ron Howard, Spike Lee, Barry Levinson, Gary Marshall, Penny Marshall, Robert Redford, Rob Reiner, John Sayles, Martin Scorsese, John Singleton, Steven Spielberg, Oliver Stone, Barbra Streisand, Quentin Tarantino, and Robert Zemeckis. All have had some formal film training before becoming directors. Several are former professional actors. Some are extremely well known, others, less so. All have produced work of merit. If you are not familiar with some of these names, I suggest that you rent their videotapes to view.

Spielberg, who studied at California State University at Long Beach, exploded onto the film scene with *Jaws*. His career is most remarkable in that he has made so few missteps and directed a highly successful string of films since his youth. Among his other features are *Close Encounters of the Third Kind*, *Raiders of the Lost Ark*, *E.T., The Extra-Terrestrial*, *The Color Purple*, *Schindler's List*, and *Amistad*. Spielberg is known for choosing highly compelling or otherwise entertaining stories and presenting them in a dynamic fashion. His career is unusual in the sense that he is both a very popular director and, especially more recently, a very critically successful one.

UCLA film school graduate Francis Ford Coppola directed the magnificent *The Godfather* trilogy, as well as *Apocalypse Now* and *The Rainmaker*, among others. Coppola seems most drawn to mythical tales of redemption and defeat, although much of his career has been devoted to lighter fare.

Martin Scorsese, a graduate of NYU, directed the innovative *Mean Streets* in 1973 shortly after graduating. He then went on to direct *Taxi Driver, Raging Bull, The King of Comedy, GoodFellas, Casino,* and *Kundun,* among others. Scorsese is known for bringing a sharp cinematic wit to his tales of the street. He uses a relentless, jarring scrutiny, along with furious cutting, slow motion, and other stylistic devices to examine the lives of those at society's dark edges. (I'm flattered that Scorsese said that my short animated film, *The Critic,* was the inspiration for his first film, *What's a Nice Girl Like you Doing in a Place Like This?*)

Born in Brooklyn, Woody Allen enrolled at NYU and City College, and was suspended from both institutions. Later he wrote sketches for the "Sid Caesar" and "Ed Sullivan" television variety shows. In writing the screenplay for *What's New, Pussycat?*, he also received his first screen role. Subsequently, Allen's work as a writer, director, and actor came to fruition. In 1977, he began to enjoy steady box-office success with a succession of popular offbeat comedies.

In the 1980s, Allen seemed to settle on the romantic comedy-drama genre. His work became imbued with a decidedly New York flavor as it explored the vicissitudes of relationships while reflecting on more serious themes. My favorite Woody Allen vehicle, *Crimes and Misdemeanors* (1989), is about a married man whose adulterous relationship leads to the cover-up of a homicide. It is full of the themes which most compel the writer/director's work: Love, guilt, integrity, and the meaning of life in the face of an inscrutable universe.

Recalling his experiences as an early movie fan in Brooklyn, Allen recounts, "When you entered the theatre you'd get this little number, and if your number came up, you would win a box of tiddlywinks. Inside the darkness, a matron with a flashlight tended the kid's section.

Then, hours later, you would feel a maternal tap on your shoulder and you'd say, "But I don't wanna go!" In his adult life, perhaps Allen has been living his dream of never leaving the movies, as he is constantly either in preproduction, production, or postproduction on a film.

Filmmaker Spike Lee graduated from the NYU Tisch School of the Arts. He directed and produced *She's Gotta Have It*, *School Daze*, *Mo' Better Blues*, *Do the Right Thing*, *Malcolm X*, and *Crooklyn*, among others. Especially notable is his engaging and fresh visual style. Lee has primarily been drawn to vignettes of African American life which blend elements of both comedy and tragedy. Perhaps one of his most arresting films is the moving documentary, *4 Little Girls*, which recalls the life of four children burned in a church basement in the 1960s.

John Singleton, a USC film writing graduate, drew notice when Columbia Pictures financed his first feature, *Boyz N the Hood*, a dramatic morality story about life in a contemporary black neighborhood. Singleton then went on to direct *Poetic Justice* and *Rosewood*, which recounts the true story of a terrible racial incident in 1920s Florida.

Barry Levinson grew up in Baltimore, Maryland. Breaking into show business as a comedy writer and performer, he won two Emmy Awards as staff writer for "The Carol Burnett Show." Then, he joined Mel Brooks's team of writers in 1977 for the movies *High Anxiety* and *History of the World—Part I*. Levinson's first directorial film effort was the highly acclaimed *Diner*, about a group of buddies who hang around a Baltimore eatery trying to deal with life and the specter of marriage. In 1988, Levinson made *Rain Man*, for which he received an Academy Award nomination as best director. In 1991, he directed the stylish gangster tale *Bugsy*. Levinson appears most drawn to stories which explore characters through their responses to highly dramatic situations.

Since directing his first low-budget film for Roger Corman, former child star of such television chestnuts as "The Andy Griffith Show" and "Happy Days," Ron Howard has directed numerous popular mainstream movies such as *Night Shift, Splash, Cocoon, Parenthood, Backdraft,* and *Apollo 13,* working in collaboration with writers such as Lowell Ganz and Babaloo Mandel. Now a seasoned director, Howard is known for his professionalism and versatility. While his early work shows a deft touch for comedy, his later work shows his ability to direct action-packed dramas with strong story lines.

Another highly versatile director who had his start in television is Rob Reiner. A former actor in television's socially relevant comedy "All in the Family," Reiner made an auspicious debut as director of the mock-documentary heavy-metal parody *This is Spinal Tap* in 1984, followed by *Stand by Me, The Princess Bride, When Harry Met Sally, Misery,* and *A Few Good Men.* Reminiscing about his first film, Reiner notes that he considered the sixty-page script for *This is Spinal Tap* as merely an outline, and subsequently almost all of the dialogue was improvised. "Often," he said, "I'd just turn on the camera and see what would happen. Then, we would alter the focus, until it felt right. The whole idea was to do a send-up of rock, but by people who loved it." Funny without being snide, the film possesses a drippy sensibility that has made it a cult classic.

A former cabaret singer and recording artist who became literally an overnight sensation in Broadway's *Funny Girl,* Barbra Streisand directed, produced, and cowrote her first feature movie, *Yentl,* in 1983. Regarding *Yentl,* Streisand says, "Not only is Isaac Bashevis's simple short story about the male and female in all of us, but it is also about facing challenges and fulfilling one's dreams." As one of the first female power brokers in Hollywood, she sees the film as a metaphor for her own career. Streisand went on to successfully direct and produce *The Prince of Tides* and *The Mirror has two Faces.*

Novelist and short-story writer John Sayles is well known as an independent American filmmaker specializing in ensemble films about ordinary people struggling with large problems. Not content to be just another film director, Sayles remarks, "I'd be happy to make a studio movie if they let me cast anybody I wanted to and gave me final cut."

The thrust of Sayles's direction revealed itself with his early feature *Matewan*, a compassionate story about a labor dispute at a coal mine in 1920s West Virginia, starkly photographed by Haskell Wexler. About *Matewan*, Sayles says, "The people I met in the hills of Kentucky and West Virginia had important stories to tell and I wanted to find a way to pass them on." Sayles continues to give voice to society's forgotten, exploring difficult social issues in films like the ironically entitled *City of Hope*, a drama that examines corruption and poverty in a troubled inner city. *Lone Star*, which Sayles both wrote and directed, smoothly combines his concerns for involving characters, local culture, and national values with the narrative drive of a thriller.

A former comedy actress on the popular television series "Laverne and Shirley," Penny Marshall has become a powerhouse director with such diverse films as *Big*, *Awakenings*, *A League of Their Own*, and *The Bishop's Wife*.

Controversial film director Oliver Stone attended NYU before directing his first low-budget feature, *Salvador*, starring James Woods. Stone then directed many argued-about films, including *JFK*, *Nixon*, and *Natural Born Killers*. His first-person account of the Vietnam War experience, *Platoon*, won several Academy Awards, including best picture and director. Regarding *Platoon*, Stone said, "I wanted to show young people what war was really like."

After studying at the Australian Film and Television School, Jane Campion directed her first feature, *Sweetie*, in 1989. Drawn to unusual stories exploring female characters, Campion wrote and directed *The Piano*, which was highly successful both critically and commercially and for which she won the Academy Award for best screenplay. The film has a disturbing quality, blending elements of romance and eroticism. Filming in her homeland of New Zealand, Campion declares, "I was after the vivid, subconscious imagery of the bush and its dark inner world."

Enjoying a successful career as an actor, Clint Eastwood made his directorial debut in 1971 with *Play Misty for Me*. After many other films, Eastwood directed *Unforgiven* in 1992, an unorthodox western that garnered several Academy Awards, including best picture and director. "I guess you can't take filmmaking too seriously," Eastwood said. "After asking my mother to be an extra in *Unforgiven*, I wound up having to cut her scene. . . and she's still pissed off at me."

Actor Robert Redford won an Academy Award with his directing debut, *Ordinary People*, a strongly acted, well-paced drama about the death of a son and its effects on a family. While living in Utah and devoting much of his time to environmental activism as well as to his association with the Sundance Film Festival, Redford continues to direct from time to time, notably the beautifully filmed tale, *A River runs Through It*.

Writer and director Quentin Tarentino made a stir with his directorial debut, *Reservoir Dogs*, and followed that up with the darkly comic *Pulp Fiction* in 1994 and *Jackie Brown* in 1997. His films generally feature a variety of interesting hit men, eccentrics, crackpots, and lowlifes, and employ a particularly stylish directorial style.

John Cassavetes, a flamboyant and well-regarded actor, made *Shadows*, his first directorial feature in 1960. The movie, shot in 16mm, is considered by film historians as a landmark in American cinema, utilizing a large degree of improvisation. Cassavetes continued to make several independent features until his death in 1989 and is widely regarded today as having been one of America's foremost independent filmmakers.

After studying animation at the California Institute of the Arts and working at the Walt Disney Studios, the multitalented Tim Burton went on to direct *Beetlejuice*, *Batman*, and *Edward Scissorhands*. In 1994 Burton directed *Ed Wood*, a sympathetic look at an eccentric B-moviemaker and his world. "I grew up watching Ed Wood's movies on television," recalls Burton. "There's something poetic about them. Wood did not let technicalities, such as visible wires and bad sets distract him. There's a twisted form of integrity to that. He didn't allow anything to discourage him." Burton too is an original, whose talents as a painter help bring his visions to life on the screen. Burton's best cinematic works are surprisingly moving fables supported by imaginative visuals.

An innovator with a strong technical flair is Robert Zemeckis. Upon graduating from the USC film school in 1984, he directed *Romancing the Stone*. He then directed the wildly successful *Back to the Future* trilogy and experimented with animation/real-life interaction in *Who Killed Roger Rabbit?* Zemeckis's highly popular fable, *Forrest Gump*, also made use of new technology to move the main character back and forth through time by his appearance in actual newsreel footage. Zemeckis states, "There seems to be a rule of thinking that if a movie has emotion or drama at its core, it cannot be entertaining."

Ethan Coen graduated from Princeton University with a degree in philosophy, while his brother Joel graduated from NYU Tisch School of the Arts. Lifelong film buffs drawn to the hilarious and the oddly sinister, they work as a team with Joel directing and Ethan producing. Among their works are *Barton Fink*, *Raising Arizona*, and *Fargo*, a droll black comedy about a murder-for-hire which garnered two Academy Awards.

ARTICLES BY GRADUATES
AND FILMMAKERS

RODNEY SCOTT, *Film Director and Screenwriter*

BRIAN YUZNA, *Film Director and Producer*

JOSEPH MANDUKE, *Filmmaker and Teacher*

KEVIN GORMAN, *Film Director and Writer*

BRENT V. FRIEDMAN, *Screenwriter and Television Producer*

MARYANNE KASICA, *Television Writer and Producer*

SHARON CINGLE, *Film Director and Screenwriter*

EDWARD DMYTRYK, *Film Director and Teacher*

BOB HOGE, *Film Director and Writer*

RODNEY SCOTT
Film Director and Screenwriter

I grew up in the ghetto frequently referred to as South Central Los Angeles. I also spent weekends in Pasadena where my father was a professional photographer. He then landed a job as an apprentice at MGM, where he continues to work.

Bused to San Fernando Valley public schools from the inner city at a young age, I eventually attended art schools. My mother vigorously searched for such schools in South Central, trying her best to keep me out of gangs. But as there weren't any special art classes in our neighborhood at that time, I began spending my days gang-banging with the brothers.

Burning with the desire to draw and create, I finally tracked down a good high school and attended art school, as well as the Los Angeles Community College, where my uncle taught a film class. Art has always been an important part of my life. I just didn't know at the time when and how it would be expressed.

I've recently completed writing and directing a 35mm dramatic feature entitled *You Ain't Gotta Lie To Kick It*, starring A.J. Johnson, Tiny Lister, and Hill Harper, as well as many more talented black actors. We shot the film on location in the neighborhood where I grew up. We also filmed in a Culver City studio, where we shot maybe eighty set-ups in twelve hours. I plan to utilize my experience from that first film for my next movie entitled *Rollin 8os*, now in preproduction.

Although I've already written three screenplays and made two short films, it is most important for me to accomplish my long-term goals. It is also crucial for me to keep things real, as well as remaining true to myself. I prefer character driven projects. Though I consider myself versatile, I choose real life stuff that can actually happen.

Sometimes I'll give my screenplay to friends on the streets to read, because when the film gets made, it will likely end up in video stores in neighborhoods like where I grew up. That's very important to me.

I'm not very analytical about myself as a young, black filmmaker. I think I'm just like every other man out there with goals and aspirations. I must continue to pursue my dreams and not give up, no matter what mood, social or economic problems I may have. In a film entitled *The Mack*, starring Max Julien, a Yale University-trained actor who plays a pimp says, "Being rich and black means something. Being poor and black don't mean shit!"

The Mack is one of my favorite movies because it portrays reality and is about fourteen brothers and sisters from the hood who show up at the theater to see that picture. It has been important for me to use my movies to say something.

After living and being around so much failure, depression, violence, joblessness, and homelessness, it shouldn't take an Ivy League professor to figure I don't want to end up like that. I'll climb the tallest building in the city I can find and scream from the rooftop at the top of my lungs: "I am somebody!" I want everybody to know it. What better way to express what I want to say? To get the message across. To have the power to create and follow my dream. To make movies and put everything in them that I wanted to say to people from that rooftop. If they didn't hear me, I'll put it in my next movie. Maybe then, it'll be something they'll want to hear. That, to me speaks to the freedom of being an independent film director.

I have received meaningful knowledge and more support from Professor Pintoff than anyone else. We met in 1992 at my first class on filmmaking at UCLA. I didn't have a clue about directing. I was basically a "fool rushing in."

Pintoff continued to council me after that particular class, not only reminding me that show business was tough, but that it would be ultimately rewarding. It seems that Pintoff never stops teaching and encouraging, and he's been an inspiration to me.

I really believe that if you put your heart and soul into something, you'll have the best chance to succeed. I have personally battled and continue to struggle. If anything, the one thing I've learned is that the fight never stops.

I feel that my career as a filmmaker is just beginning. Nobody knows who I am. But I'll never take my eyes off the prize, and hope it's only a matter of time before everybody sees my movies.

BRIAN YUZNA
Film Director and Producer

I never intended to become a filmmaker. Majoring in Comparative Religion as well as Art in college would hardly seem to be the preparation for a career in the movies. But as it turned out, it wasn't until I was in my mid-thirties, after having tried various occupations, that I decided to go to Hollywood and produce movies.

The only preparation I had was watching films as a hard–core fan. Because it was my favorite genre, I produced my first film, a horror movie, based on H.P. Lovecraft's book entitled *Re–Animator*. Fortunately, the film did well enough to save me from financial ruin because I was able to pay back all the money I had borrowed. I really didn't make any profit from the film, although it had achieved critical success in the mainstream media and became a consensus cult classic in the genre. It did, however, teach me how to make a commercial movie as well as providing a school of hard knocks in the biz and its legal aspects. After five years of lawsuits, I more or less broke even on the project. Although this may seem to be the standard cautionary tale about the pitfalls in Hollywood, to me it isn't. My aim was to make movies that others would find interesting. It is *Re-Animator* that made it possible for me to enjoy a career in the movie business.

I started out as a movie producer because I was led to believe that the producer was most powerful and that he made the most money. But I soon learned that the director has all the fun. As a director, you are often rewriting the script, so it is natural to become involved in writing, too. As a matter of fact, because I have originated and developed all my projects, writing and collaboration are inevitable. Basically, I read every book I could find on the subject of financing, organizing, and shooting before I started making movies myself.

83

With enough talent, strength of vision, and filmmaking know-how, a director can almost qualify as an auteur. This is true despite the collaborative nature of filmmaking. Although a film, at its best, should express the single vision of the artist, making a movie necessitates the working together of creative talents and technicians. This, in fact, drew me to working in that media.

I have never had a mentor in the traditional sense of the term, which does not mean I think teachers can't be valuable. On the contrary, I believe that an apprenticeship, whether in the classroom or the workplace, is the best place to learn.

Because I entered the movie business later in life than many others, I missed out on that experience. When I did indeed begin to direct, I discovered myself often referring to other movies for inspiration. That became increasingly important to me and I began to actively turn to the classics. In a way, the early filmmakers served as my mentors, especially the works of Fritz Lang, Joseph Von Sternberg, Eric Von Stroheim, Sergei Eisenstein, and Alfred Hitchcock.

Producing films presents its own unique challenges, but finally, for me, it is joined at the hip with directing and writing. It is all about inventing a movie. Ideally, producing movies involves organizing the production from concept through release. The producer is there at the very beginning.

Although I created *Honey, I Shrunk the Kids*, it ultimately became a highly collaborative project. If you only direct, you may never get the opportunity to collaborate with other directors who can be some of the most remarkable and stimulating people in the business. As a producer, collaborating with directors has deepened my understanding of both style and technique. I have produced for many first-time directors as well as experienced ones and I have learned from them all.

To successfully produce movies, it is important to get inside the directors' head so that you can help them realize their aesthetic. For me, I must feel as though I can effectively solve problems on their terms, not mine.

I find that the most effective way to internalize the aesthetics of other directors is to watch the films that have been important to them because these are directly influencing your present project.

One of the most efficient ways of communicating, whether in tone, framing, or editing, is to refer to other films that may contain similar elements. The simplest example of this is the movie pitching technique that was prevalent in the eighties. One would say that a script was a cross between two previous usually very successful films. For example, "*Under Siege* is really *Die Hard* on a ship." I have found that many successful directors have fascinating film vocabularies. After all, the language of cinema is film. That has spurred me to expand my own filmic resources when I direct and has led me to a have a voracious appetite for film history.

For the past several years, I have spent hours watching old movies and reading film history books, especially the early stuff from the twenties and thirties. I have also found that silent films offer a wealth of emotion, both aesthetically and in solid storytelling.

There is something exhilarating about studying the origins of the film medium as a narrative art form. It is enlightening to interpret the contemporary cinema with a clear perspective, because most of the techniques employed were pioneered over seventy years ago. Those early films in fact give me a boost when I direct. The genre is usually fantasy, action, and horror. One thing that continues to surprise me about silent films is how genre they actually are. Except for the epics, genre films often deal with moral and spiritual tensions in an atmospheric or expressionistic style. That is what genre fans like myself enjoy in movies.

Familiarity with those early masterworks helps me to look past the spectacle of light and sound that often enriches storytelling in contemporary films. Concentrating on emotion, style, and ideas should always be the enduring core of cinema.

JOSEPH MANDUKE
Filmmaker and Teacher

Film directing is easy. Receiving a firm commitment to direct a picture is what lies beyond the realm of reason for a new entrant into the motion picture marketplace, unless you have a relative who likes you or runs a studio, or a major star insists that you alone are the director, or you alone control a brilliant screenplay with you attached as the director.

Having laid down that caveat, I sincerely want to advise and encourage all film students to pursue a career in film directing for movies and television. It is a unique and wonderful place to be active. A great percentage of the world's population have embraced film as a universal language. Just imagine being part of a performing art that might be translated into every language and viewed by millions of people. It is conceivable that you can reach out with your own imagination and ideas, put them on film, and change someone's life in a far-off place.

Give people hope, spirit them forward, display the truths and injustices that exist. By all means, make them laugh. Movies can be as entertaining as they can be provocative. The choices are yours to make. Why wouldn't anyone want to be in an industry that portends to have all these qualities?

If you are passionate in your choice and tenacious in your goal to direct, and if you have a confident sense of your own talent as well as being emotionally prepared for rejection, then go for it. It can be a fascinating and challenging career. Interesting people, exotic locations, and a full active life lie ahead, with a few roadblocks of course. But that's part of the fun.

Recently, I had the opportunity to supervise and mentor a full-length, industry standard 35mm film at a leading West Coast university, made possible by a grant. The core participants were postgraduate film students and the purpose of the program was to create an atmosphere for graduates to experience, hands-on, the process of script-to-screen production.

The result exceeded my expectations and, in retrospect, I believe the success of the film, in part, was due to the students' ability to interact and collaborate on several levels. The group, from the very beginning, understood and agreed that there was one leader, the director.

The director, in turn, comprehended the need for input from his team. They had many surprises and several disagreements, but ultimately the scripted characters transcended the differences, along with thanks to skillful directing and brilliant casting. I'm pleased to report that a large percentage of the participants are now working in the entertainment industry and will hopefully achieve their goals.

Obviously, having a degree in film, albeit one of the best ingredients to help build a foundation of knowledge, is not an automatic E-Ticket to success.

Now that you've learned the basic rules, go forth and break them. Improvise and let your own imagination, storytelling ability, and cine-matic ingenuity and energy propel you to create your own opportunities.

I strongly suggest that you produce a showcase of your talent as a direc-tor and when you are ready with an idea, story, or script, assemble a core group of associates who may contribute and assist you with your first effort. No matter if it's a short or full-length film, get it done and make the end product as brilliant as possible. It could be the golden key to opening doors to agents, studios, distributors, lawyers, managers, and actors who may help you land a plum directing assignment. Collaborate with your team. Put together a shooting schedule and budget. A rigorously professional presentation is required to obtain financing for your project. The pressures are great, but not insurmountable.

Finally, If you want it badly enough, I feel confident it will happen.

KEVIN GORMAN
Film Director and Writer

I can only describe the look on my parents' faces when I told them I wanted to be a movie director as some combination of loving encouragement and horror. The combination could not have been more appropriate.

Encouragement, because they are great parents and would not want to deny me my dreams, and horror because they had some intuitive grasp of how hard it is to work as a director. Short of having an extremely well-connected family, there is no way to guarantee a break into the movie business.

As for me, I was an English major in college with a strong interest in film, so I moved to Los Angeles and enrolled at the University of Southern California.

While some people will belittle the idea of studying movies, there are some useful things to learn at film school. One of them is a basic technical understanding of how cameras, lenses, and film work together to capture an image. That is important because part of being a good filmmaker is learning to control light and the moods it can create.

A second thing you can brush up on is film history. Having the chance to analyze some great movies in depth and to understand what makes them work will open your eyes to the possibilities of film. And last, but by no means least, you will get an opportunity to practice the craft of filmmaking. If you are lucky, you'll get a chance to take a directing course like the one taught by Ernest Pintoff.

Professor Pintoff's course was called Directing the Mise En Scène, and there were usually about sixteen aspiring filmmakers in a class. He would divide the class into groups of four. Each group would then become crew members in which all students would alternate as director, cinematographer, dolly grip, and sound person.

When it was the your turn to direct, you were responsible for picking a scene, casting the actors, and building the set.

Professor Pintoff wanted his students to feel the pressure under which a professional director has to work. To accomplish that end he insisted that your scene be shot within a one-hour time constraint. This simple rule taught would-be directors the importance of preparation. Mostly, the professor nurtured and encouraged students. His wrath was reserved for those who did not take the assignment seriously.

That class also taught the importance of decisiveness. Pintoff felt strongly that you must make your choices and stand by them, even if you have to take a little heat. In this class, student directors had to know what they wanted to do with the scene and had to be ready to meet the daily challenges to their authority.

Later in my film school career, I directed a short film with my class-mates working as crew. I learned a great deal from this process, though trying to tell film students what to do is like herding cats. The students are convinced they can do a better job and no one wants to do the dirty work. With no three picture deal on the horizon, I packed away my riding crops and ascots and I did the unthinkable: I got a job.

I guess I'm lucky in one respect, since my day job is in show biz. After completing film school, I found work making behind–the–scenes documentaries about current feature films in production. While this is not necessarily where I want to end up, it has been an interesting place to start. I have the opportunity to see professional filmmakers at work and I can see how they solve the challenges of directing a film on time and on budget while trying to produce something people will remember.

One lesson becomes very clear: It takes as much energy to make a bad movie as it does to make a good movie. Most importantly, through the course of these productions, I get to talk to the actors, the producers, and the directors and ask them what they're trying to accomplish. When I am on the set, I try to understand how the directors are shooting their scene and what I can learn from these people or their approach, or maybe how I would shoot it differently. When it's all over, I get to ask if they are happy with the result.

Of all the sets I have been on and all the directors I have observed, it never ceases to amaze me how the simple rules I learned in Professor Pintoff's class are proven true again and again. Nothing beats good preparation and nothing is more important than having a solid script, ideally before production begins.

Of course you don't have to go to film school to become a director. One can learn a huge amount about procedure and protocol on the job just by being part of a working crew. You probably won't be starting as the director, but that's okay. The film business has a long tradition of allowing people to work their way up. If you aren't too obnoxious, you might even find someone who can answer your questions. I heard of one guy who made the leap on a low-budget feature from helping craft services to directing second-unit in the span of three weeks. Granted, the production was in chaos, but you know what the Chinese say about crisis and opportunity: "A crisis never seems like an opportunity when it's happening." It might merely be your "big break."

Even if you aren't yet working on a film set, there is still much you can do to teach yourself about directing. Start watching movies as a director. Figure out why a director approaches a scene in a certain way. Try to understand why the director decided to use a certain camera angle or sound effect.

93

Remember that a director is trying to affect you emotionally, to make you feel something or think something special. What movie moments have affected you? Begin to analyze why they worked. In essence, create your own film school. Meet with other people, if possible, who share your passion for film and discuss your ideas. The next step is obtaining a camera.

Though the paths that have allowed many people to become filmmakers are varied, there is a common tenacity of purpose in the people I have met. Whatever their reasons, they were determined to become directors. Some came from television, others from producing, screenwriting, or from the families of the well connected. They face the same two problems you do. Where do you put the camera and what do you tell the actors? You might start thinking about the answers now because once production begins, you won't have a moment to yourself. Everybody will want to talk to you and hopefully you won't have to struggle to keep your priorities straight, even as they are asking where you want your trailer positioned and how much nutmeg you take with your cappuccino.

BRENT V. FRIEDMAN
Screenwriter and Television Producer

Collaboration, a word every good director must believe in. By its very definition, film production is a collaborative medium.

Gaffers, grips, and location scouts, a whole cast of characters and technicians, are hired to bring your vision to light. You become omnipotent. You are the brain trust. You are the guiding light. But is it solely your vision?

Writing, unlike directing, generally requires no support team. It is a noncollaborative endeavor. Imagine a pregnant mother alone in some isolated cabin in the woods midwifing her child into existence. It's no wonder every writer feels overly possessive of his vision. But films, when not written and directed by the same person, can suffer greatly from double vision. The child who receives opposing orders from both parents will probably turn out to be schizophrenic.

Now that we know the players, let's examine the process. Traditionally, once a screenplay is sold, developed, boarded, budgeted, and rushed into production, the writer's precious work, his child, is unceremoniously torn from his arms and turned over to its new legal guardian, the director. All those sleepless nights, the frustration of trying to inspire his script to untold greatness, all those days of toil are now traded in for money. Sounds like your typical divorce, right? It is without even a memory of the good times, unless a writer has been fortunate enough to have his script given to a benevolent spirit, or a director who actually collaborates.

Over the years as a feature writer, I have had varying experiences and it's hard to imagine there could be a situation I haven't yet encountered.

Thrown from the set? Been there. Flown to Israel, first class, no less, to rewrite on the set? Done that. Each experience was completely unique and contingent upon the marriage of the two most important minds on a production—the writer and director. Other crew members may be on a different page, but if those two key players are not in sync, all the gorgeous photography and sumptuous sets cannot save your film. Truly, it's all about ego.

I'll let you in on a little secret. Every word a writer types into his script is there for a reason. Seriously. Everything, down to the most insignif-icant-seeming comma, has been unduly fretted over. That is certainly not to say that every word or line of dialogue has equal merit. Far from it. I believe that it is the director's job to analyze every word of the script and rather than dismissing everything that doesn't coincide with his view, a good director will spend countless hours developing a script with his writer.

Additionally, it is incumbent for a good writer to separate the wheat from the chaff when a director's notes spew forth over the fax, a dreaded moment for even the most hardened of scribes. A writer must embrace the good and tactfully argue against the bad. It is simply not enough to proclaim a life-threatening allergy to wheat.

Open-mindedness is a sentiment that will not only foster a wonderful working relationship between the most influential minds on every pro-duction, but the script will rightly prosper. Mutual respect is the name of the game. Remember, every child needs two parents, preferably living happily under the same roof.

Recently having crossed over into television, where writers often function as producers, too, I found myself in a position to hire the director to bring my very words to life.

Would I seek an automaton to execute my bidding without so much as a whimper or would I hire a respected and sought–after visionary to take over? Because I was the producer, the mediator if you will, I decided for something unique. I wanted both. Someone to shape the script into something even better than was on the page and someone to acknowledge that it was our vision. Deep down, I believe this is what every writer dreams of.

Reading the reviews of my produced shows, I have found that those without real collaboration suffered most in the translation from page to screen. Hopefully, aspiring directors will come to learn that trust, respect, and communication are all necessary ingredients of a positive working relationship, a lesson that may even be applied to your personal life. But that's another book.

Writers and directors both enter their blind date with fear and trepidation; each tries to establish dominance, then clings to the mountaintop with fierce determination. Unfortunately, the good of the script is often sacrificed in the pursuit of childish self-interest. So, if you forget everything else you read in these pages, bear in mind the words of a wise soul whose name now escapes me: "The script is the thing!"

MARYANNE KASICA
Television Writer and Producer

I fell in love when I was in the third grade while watching a visiting group of actors perform *Hansel and Gretel*. How wonderful I thought and from then on gave my heart over to the theater.

Subsequently, I became fascinated by movies and their glamour. Television, with its immediacy and easy access, won me over as well. One has to be enraptured with show business to have a career in it, because it is so demanding and heartbreaking, while promising great joy and thrills.

After graduating from Fairleigh Dickinson University with a B.A. in English Literature, I acquired my Equity card in summer stock, and then ventured to New York City in order to pursue a career in acting. Once there, I studied, appeared in workshop performances, made the rounds, and auditioned. The only writing at that time was for my own pleasure.

I married and moved to Los Angeles, then enrolled at Cal State, where I earned my Master of Arts degree in Drama. While working for my degree, I took several directing classes that helped me both as an actress and writer.

Inasmuch as the entertainment industry is a collaborative one, it helps to acquire experience in every aspect of it. Fortunately, everything I have done in summer stock, such as acting, film workshops, film classes, and performing on sound stages of movies and television shows has paid off.

I started writing monologues and one-character plays to perform in theater workshops. Everyone was very enthusiastic about my writing but not about my acting. So, it became easier to find work as a writer than as an actress. The competition was not as keen, though getting in the door was just as difficult.

As a writer, I get to imagine playing all the characters. I can also picture how it feels to direct and shoot while writing the script. Once my work is finished and given to the director my involvement shifts from creator to collaborator.

Mostly I write murder mysteries and thriller teleplays, having written for "Hart To Hart," Magnum, P.I.," "Murder She Wrote," "Matlock," "Silk Stalkings," "Time Trax," and others.

As a television writer I have limited interaction with the director. Generally, the network, production company, and producer wield the final power and influence of a show's content. But I usually have one or two creative meetings dealing with rewrites. That is where the director's vision and mine are either in conflict or in complete agreement.

Often a director's impulse may invigorate a scene or sequence that has the writer stumped. If the director likes the script enough to do it, chances are that both the writer and director are in sync, and collaborating on rewrites is a pleasure. If the director doesn't like the script but elects to work on it anyway, it is likely that the work process will become more negotiation than collaboration.

Normally in television, the director shoots just what is on the page, the major considerations being budget and schedule. Artistry often gives way to time pressure, and creativity to budget constraints.

What I enjoy about television is that the chance of your work being produced is greater than in features where many extraneous factors influence the final go-ahead.

As a woman, I find that my point of view is both welcomed and ignored. I cannot honestly say that there has ever been any pointed rejection of any idea or contribution I have offered based on gender. It may exist, but show business is so competitive, one can only assume work is accepted or rejected on its own merit.

SHARON CINGLE
Film Director and Screenwriter

I was never one of those kids who knew just what I was going to do when I grew up. I wasn't a sick kid who spent all day in my room drawing images, nor was I a superambitious child who made several short films before the age of ten. In fact, the only movie I can remember seeing at the drive-in was *Xanadu*.

Although it never sparked my interest in filmmaking, *Xanadu* did make me dream about becoming Olivia Newton John on roller skates.

I soon abandoned that dream after discovering I was no good as a blonde and even worse as a roller skater. I never even thought about filmmaking as a career until, out of curiosity, I took a couple of eight millimeter film classes at a community college in San Francisco. After that, I was hooked and knew that I wanted to write and direct.

There I was, yearning to write and direct without a clue as to how to go about it. I believed that getting a job on a movie would be a great start, but I soon learned that the classified section of the *San Francisco Herald Examiner* wasn't exactly the best place to look.

I asked a fellow classmate if he had any idea how I might break into the film industry. He slowly lifted his Kool cigarette and exhaled through his nose while mumbling about Hollywood being totally fucked and that it wasn't what you know, it's who you know and that I had to meet the right people.

I shook my head as though I understood, then asked how one got to meet those people. Annoyed, he took one last hit on his cigarette before flinging the butt away and said I should just get a job in the film

103

industry and what was this anyway, Film Job Search 101? It all seemed terribly difficult.

Confused and frustrated with the job situation, I figured that film school was the next best thing. Attending the University of Southern California was a valuable learning experience which was enjoyable at times, frustrating at other times, and very competitive.

I found the biggest advantage of film school is that you are surrounded by students who are interested in doing the same things you are. Showing your work in class, you are open to criticism and comments that might be helpful to your work.

Sometimes you might storm out of class feeling miserable, though other times you can feel as high as a kite because your idea came across the way you wanted. I have since discovered that one of the greatest gifts to have is learning to follow your instincts and knowing when to take the criticism or when to leave it at the door.

I do not believe it is necessary to earn a degree from a university if you want to work in the film industry. But I do believe that it is essential to study the films of others, learn from their successes and failures, and use that technical knowledge when creating your own personal works.

If you think that film school is necessary then you may be fortunate to encounter a professor like Ernest Pintoff, who shows you how to see things new and differently, though keeping himself open to new ideas.

I never felt like we were in a classroom; it seemed like we were on a journey searching for some hidden truth. If you find a mentor who inspires you, don't hesitate to learn from him or her.

On the other hand, if film school is not for you, there are other ways to learn the trade. One path would be to make your own film, as my friend and I chose to do when we collaborated on a 16mm low-budget feature entitled *Yeah, OK, Whatever. . .*

Making that movie was a commitment I hadn't anticipated would take so long. Three years in the making and facing the biggest problem that is inevitable to all filmmakers, finding the financing. While holding down steady jobs, we shot for an entire summer, averaging four days a week. Trying to scrape the money together to finish the movie, we were maxing out our credit cards, and inspired by Spike Lee, spent our student loans and swallowed our pride as we begged for money.

I recommend that anyone wishing to make a low-budget movie first get to know the equipment. I cannot count the number of expensive mistakes that could have been prevented had we familiarized ourselves with the equipment.

Realize how much of a commitment it truly is and that every cent you make will be put toward the film. There will be many sacrifices, such as time, money, and sleep. But you must be willing to give up everything with the risk that your film may never even be seen. If you are smarter than we were, you might find a source to finance your film; if not, I still say go for it. Making *Yeah, OK, Whatever. . .* was a struggle, but it was also one of the best experiences of my life.

If you want to write and direct, there are many methods you can choose to learn your craft, whether it be attending a school, going the independent route, or working on films.

Honing your filmmaking skills is important, but what is more important is the idea. Coming up with a good idea is not something that is taught; it is something that is most often acquired through years of living. As a filmmaker, you must act like a sponge, soaking up your experiences. Observe and absorb all that you can about the nature of human beings. Search always for the hidden truths that lie deep inside of us. This core, this truth, should drive you, the filmmaker, so much that the need to express it should intoxicate you. So, as you budding filmmakers struggle to make it in Hollywood, I leave you with these words of advice: Never take the business too seriously. Always be true to yourself, and never ever give up hope.

EDWARD DMYTRYK
Film Director and Teacher

The somewhat unusual circumstances of my life and career permit me to discuss film education only from an instructor's point of view. I have never been a film student in the narrow sense of the term.

Nineteen twenty-three was the year I started working as a messenger boy at Famous Players Lasky, which eventually became Paramount Pictures. At the age of fourteen I left home and was working my way through high school. By the summer of that year I had wormed my way into the projection rooms and eventually became a studio projectionist.

I had no intention of making film my career. I was a mathematician, and a scholarship allowed me to enroll at Cal Tech where I planned to major in mathematical physics. But I continued working at my projectionist job on weekends, and by the end of a year, I decided to make motion pictures my life's work. What changed my mind was a perception that the directors, producers, and actors whom I met as a projectionist were much more interesting than those people I had associated with outside the studio environment. The imminent arrival of "sound" may have been another incentive.

From June 1927, I worked full time in the projection booths, and when "talkies" became a part of the film scene, I negotiated a transfer to the editorial department. Within a few months I became a full-time film editor.

After ten years of editing for directors such as Leo McCarey and George Cukor, I was asked to take over the direction of a B movie. From 1939 to my semiretirement in 1978 I directed, and occasionally produced, fifty-seven features, seventeen of which were Bs, the rest As.

In 1978 I started teaching at the University of Texas at Austin. In 1981, I came to USC, where I have been teaching a full schedule until the present day.

It may seem odd that I was not hooked on films during my first four years at the studio, or that when I finally chose filmmaking as a career, I had no vision, no dream, no real idea of exactly what I wanted to do. I had only a highly competitive nature, a desire to excel at everything I did, and an unusual but well-rounded education. I was an autodidact, with a catholic interest in the human condition.

Although I became a director by accident, I realize that I had the best possible preparation for the job—internship with great directors. The only thing in question was the presence of the special talent required, and there was no way to test that except in the fire. It follows that I consider apprenticeship the best way to learn not only the fundamentals, but especially the esoterica of any art. Today, of course, such opportunities are rare if they exist at all. With no professional feedback to monitor their passage, thousands of aspiring young visionaries matriculate at hundreds of colleges and universities to learn all there is to know about filmmaking except those things that a good filmmaker must know.

I sometimes mystify my students by admitting that I don't know how to load a camera or set a light. I never had to do either of those things. Skilled experts in those fields did them for me. A proper education, not technique and mechanical expertise, is the secret of good filmmaking. Let me quote two sources to make my point. Speaking of college students, Norman Cousins wrote: "They are beautifully skilled, but intellectually underdeveloped. They know everything there is to know about the human situation that serves as the context for their work." And that great ballet star Baryshnikov said: "We are a lost generation, a lot of people who are aggressive and virtuosic but have little inside." I ask, "Where is the soul?"

People more interested in education than I have said that few of today's university students are truly educated. And very few of those whose hearts are set on cinema recognize that creative filmmaking requires the study of many disciplines that have nothing to do with films directly. These disciplines concern human belief, human history, human behavior, human character, and human intercommunication. In short, all aspects of human nature. And none of these has anything to do with the mechanics of filmmaking.

Of course the more skillful the techniques the better the presentation, and these are well taught at most film schools. But if such skills were indispensable some of our greatest filmmakers would never have been allowed to expose a foot of film. On the other hand, if the characters and the contexts of their work had been shallow, all the techniques available would not have made their films live. Only a deep understanding of life could do that, and it seems that a mere handful of students seek the real sources of such understanding.

The student must realize that although he can learn the basic techniques of filmmaking in a few months, he cannot learn all he should know about the characters who inhabit his films and the problems that beset them in a hundred years. But by God, he should try.

In addition to writing six technical books on film, my directing credits include *Hitler's Children*; *Murder, my Sweet*; *Till the End of Time*; *Crossfire*; *Christ in Concrete*; *The Caine Mutiny*; *Broken Lance*; *The End of the Affair*; *Raintree County*; *The Young Lions*; *Warlock*; *A Walk on the Wild Side*; *The Carpetbaggers*; and *Mirage*.

BOB HOGE
Film Director and Writer

I begin with a bit of stunning news: Hollywood is a rough place. I have personally experienced the tough side of Los Angeles, moving here ten years ago in search of a dream and encountering mostly rejection letters.

After all that time and all that rejection I have finally learned the secret. It is a secret that I have previously learned and will doubtless have to be learned again because it is a secret that is easy to forget.

In the immortal words of a sneaker manufacturer, "Just do it." Don't wait for someone to help you, because it's up to you. In Hollywood, potential is cheap, only results count.

I learned this lesson in Ernie Pintoff's first class. Frustrated with my stalled screenwriting career, I enrolled in a directing course at the UCLA Extension and soon found myself face-to-face with Professor Pintoff.

Before I could sink into my chair, put my feet up, and start the *Daily Bruin* crossword puzzle, Pintoff announced to the assembled throng that students would be required to bring in rehearsed scenes, complete with actors, and present them in class.

I blanched. Was he nuts? I just wanted to sit in the back row and learn a few things, at least not make an ass of myself in front of strangers.

The presentations would consist of simulating the directing process, Pintoff continued, going through all the steps except the actual exposing of film. We would be required to bring in shot lists, discuss our

111

chosen camera angles, and work with the actors to achieve the best performances.

I was annoyed. I was shocked. I was scared and peeked at my watch. When was the first break? I would saunter toward the men's room, slip out the back door, and call the registrar tomorrow to let her know that I'd come down with some dreaded disease and would not be attending Pintoff's class.

You see, it was one thing to think about directing, to talk about directing, and to plan about directing, but it was another thing to do it, especially in a pressure situation in front of a whole class and a sharp-eyed professor. A pressure situation that would be just like a movie set.

But Professor Pintoff didn't take a break. In fact, he made the students sign up for their directing slots. As Pintoff went through the list, he noticed that I hadn't signed up.

"I'm just, uh, auditing," I muttered, acutely conscious of the fact that everyone seemed to be peering at me. A bead of sweat appeared on my brow.

Pintoff wasn't impressed. "Auditing is not allowed," he explained. Besides, how could I expect to get anything out of the class unless I participated? With that line of thought, he promptly assigned me to a slot for the following week.

At home later that night, I still desperately wanted to drop out, but now my pride was involved. I had to go through with it. Already, I had made the mistake of telling my girlfriend about my dilemma. Now, if I begged out, she would have no choice but to conclude that I was an intolerable wimp. Case closed.

I swallowed my fear, searched through plays, found a scene, started calling actors, and the following week I actually had a scene. I stood before the class, asked the actors to take their places, cleared my throat and called, "Action!"

You know what? I actually lived through the experience.

After I finished, the professor and the students critiqued my work. You might think that directing actors in front of an audience without a camera or crew would have nothing to do with filmmaking. Not so. Pintoff had us indicate where the camera would be for the different angles, where we would move in for coverage and close-ups as well as how the scene would be dressed and lit. While the technical aspects were addressed, I found that his approach allowed me to focus on the most important aspect of directing the actors. I recall Pintoff pointing out that a stage performance may require vocal projection, but film acting is based on subtle qualities such as nuance, body language, and facial expression.

I urge aspiring directors to take an acting class. Fortunately, I have had some acting experience; when I directed my first feature film, I found that having some knowledge of acting techniques enabled me to elicit the performances I wanted. No matter how many special effects, spectacular stunts, or ingenious lighting set-ups your film contains, the audience will most likely be gaping at thirty-foot–high human faces for much of the time. If they don't care about the people behind those faces, they are unlikely to care about the movie. But the lesson I learned that first night in class is one that I keep learning over and over again in Hollywood. If you want something, go get it. Want to write? Sit down, shut up, and start writing. Want to produce? Pick up the phone. Want to direct? Get a camera.

Don't wait for some studio to hand you their next movie. It will never happen. Can't finance a feature? Make a short. Can't make a short? Make a videotape. Make a reel. Find a way and make it happen. Sure, it's scary. In fact, it's terrifying. But what is the alternative?

Since that first class when Ernest was so heartless, forcing me to direct a scene, I have swallowed my fear and have since directed my first feature film that I also produced.

By the time you read this, my movie will either be a success or a failure. But you know, I don't really care. In either case, it's been more fun than sitting in the back row doing a crossword puzzle.

OBSERVATIONS

The following photos and personal observations are from feature and television films that I have directed over the span of my film-making career.

While directing *Harvey Middleman, Fireman*, my first feature, I quickly learned the importance of being patient. In this instance, the tempera-mental cat I selected did not wish to go for her platter of milk

directing *Harvey Middleman, Fireman*

directing tempermental kitten

on cue. Stymied while precious moments passed, I was forced to wait until the prima donna feline was good and ready. Although I believe that directing requires talent and many skills, I also know from experience that it has a great deal to do with patience.

Directing children requires different considerations. Communicating with kids must be simple and clear. Children must, by law, be supervised by a teacher while filming in order to insure their well-being and continu-ing education. In general, I welcome parents to be on set while their chil-dren are performing. Their help and support is often an asset.

directing children

115

Regarding the calling of "Action!" I believe that the director is the only one on set to assert that command. During the filming of a stunt or when background action is called for, the first AD should call, "Background Action!" before the "Action" command of the director. The same applies to the calling of "Cut!" That command is given only by the director. It should be remembered to allow an extra amount of time at the end of a scene before giving that command. During editing, the director, composer, and/or editor often wish they had some precious extra seconds. After a take, it is wise to record ambient sound for possible use in mixing.

Working with stunt men in potentially dangerous scenes is always hazardous. The success of this scene from *St. Helens* required close com-

munication with the cast, crew and stunt gaffer.

Directing complex special effects sequences called for in television's "Call to Glory" necessitated precise interaction with cast and crew.

directing stunts on *St. Helens*

directing special effects on *Call to Glory*

116

RECOMMENDED BOOKS AND FILMS

The following is a list of recommended books and films:

RECOMMENDED BOOKS

Adventures in the Screen Trade, by William Goldman; Warner Books.

The Complete Film Dictionary, by Ira Koningsberg; the Penguin Group.

The Complete Guide to Standard Script Forms, by Cole and Haag; CMC Publishing.

Directing the Film, by Eric Sherman; Acrobat Books.

The Filmmaker's Handbook, by Edward Pincus and Steven Ascher; the Penguin Group.

Final Cut, by Stephen Bach; William Morrow.

Hollywood Rajah, by Bosley Crowther; Holt, Rinehart and Winston.

Picture, by Lillian Roth; Dolphin Books.

Scorsese on Scorsese, edited by David Thompson and Ian Christie; Faber and Faber.

The Timetables of History, by Bernard Grun; Touchstone Publishing.

RECOMMENDED FILMS

Amadeus, directed by Milos Forman; Orion Pictures.

Crimes and Misdemeanors, directed by Woody Allen; Orion Pictures.

East of Eden, directed by Elia Kazan; Warner Bros.

The Big Picture, directed by Christopher Guest; Columbia TriStar.

The Four Hundred Blows, directed by Francois Truffaut; Zenith International.

The Godfather, directed by Francis Ford Coppola; Paramount Pictures.

Lawrence of Arabia, directed by David Lean; Columbia Pictures.

The Lion in Winter, directed by Anthony Harvey; Embassy Pictures.

Manhattan, directed by Woody Allen; United Artists.

Mean Streets, directed by Martin Scorsese; Warner Bros.

Paper Moon, directed by Peter Bogdanovich; Paramount Pictures.

The Player, directed by Robert Altman; New Line Cinema.

Radio Days, directed by Woody Allen; Orion Pictures.

GLOSSARY

A and B ROLL EDITING

A and B roll printing contains alternating segments of the original film that overlap each other when dissolves are required. The A and B technique enables dissolves and fades to be effected without going through another processing generation.

A and B ROLL PRINTING

A and B roll printing is accomplished with two or more rolls of film, conformed and matching, with alternate scenes intercut with black leader. This process allows for checkerboard cutting that eliminates visual film splices on the screen. It also permits single or double exposures, multiple exposure, and hands-on reediting by the frame.

ABOVE-THE-LINE

Above-the-line refers to the portion of budget that includes producer, director, actors, script, and writer, considered to be the creative elements, including the major talent and the property itself. The separation is made between such expenses and all others, referred to as below-the-line, because often the above-the-line costs will be deferred, particularly regarding talent, who often participate in the profits or gross revenues of the film.

AMBIENT SOUND

The natural environmental noise, or ambient sound, that surrounds a scene. Usually, environmental noises have their own sound track for mixing.

ANIMATION CAMERA

Used for filming animation, this camera is usually mounted on a stand with its optical axis vertical so that it looks down on the objects being photographed. The camera-drive meter allows the film to move forward one frame at a time.

ANIMATION STAND or ANIMATION CRANE

An animation stand, or animation crane, is a precise, customized camera mount for animation usage. This stand or crane is capable of accurate gradations of movement above the art work, peg board or platen, and usually has capabilities for both subtle and complex moves.

ANIMATION TABLE

An animation table consists of a circular rotary inset. This transparent surface permits the cel to be turned to any angle for observations, matching, inking, or painting.

ARMORER

On a movie set, the armorer is the person in charge of weapons and their ammunition.

ARRIFLEX

The Arriflex camera is a 16mm camera commonly used for newsgathering, industrials, commercials, and documentaries; 35mm models are also utilized for commercials, high-budget documentaries, and industrial films, as well as for feature motion pictures. Feature movies, or parts of features, are also shot on 16mm formats, then optically blown up to 35mm.

ASSOCIATE PRODUCER

The associate producer gets generally involved in preproduction, production and postproduction. He primarily aids and supports the producer. This function and credit is sometimes given to a production manager or first assistant director for contributions that exceed their routine duties.

AUTEUR

This French word means "author" and in film perceives the director as the controlling entity of a film, as an artist who infuses the entire work with his personality and point of view and all of whose films can be related in terms of similar techniques, style, and themes.

AVANT-GARDE CINEMA

A French phrase meaning "the advanced group in cinema," it refers to experimental, nonlinear and noncommercial moviemaking.

BEAULIEU

A 16mm lightweight motion picture camera, the Beaulieu is used extensively for news and documentary coverage.

BELOW-THE-LINE

Below-the-line refers to those figures in the budget that accrue after the film has begun. For example, expenses for crew, shooting, editing, and all production activities. This category may also include salaries not contractually agreed upon before shooting begins as part of the above-the-line costs.

BLANK SHELL

A blank shell is a powder-filled cartridge with no projectile.

BLAXPLOITATION FILMS

Commercial-minded films of the 1970s that capitalized on the drawing power of action films with black heroes became known as blax-
ploitation films. The design of these films exploited the popularity of
black actors in screen stories that were often highly sensational.
Crime plots with a superhero figure, such as the movie *Shaft*, directed
by Gordon Parks in 1971, were common ingredients. Additional titles
within the genre include *Superfly*, *Melinda*, *TNT*, *Black Belt Jones*, *Three
the Hard Way*, and *Coffey*, all filmed in the early seventies.

BLOW-UP

To blow-up, or to optically blow-up is to make a larger duplicate picture from a smaller gauge. It is possible to make an optical blow-up
of a 16mm format to a 35mm format while still maintaining sufficient
quality and definition for public release.

BOOM

A boom is a long, mobile, telescopic arm with a microphone attached
at one end that is usually held over an actor's head outside the camera's
frame. The boom follows the characters and permits synchronous
sound recording of the filmed scene.

B-PICTURE

The B-picture describes a movie that commonly appeared as the second film on a double-feature bill in the thirties, forties, and fifties. It's
budget was markedly less than that of the main picture, sometimes
known as the A-picture. This was reflected in the film through its use

of lesser-known stars and reworked plots, often drawn from familiar genres such as science fiction or westerns. Though an object of scorn for many years, such films became of interest to film historians and popular culture enthusiasts as reflections of period attitudes and mores. Some B-pictures have achieved cult status for a variety of qualities such as quirkiness, innocence, comic undertones, or innovations in subject matter or technique.

BREAKAWAY

A breakaway refers to a property or part of the set made to break away easily without injury to the performer. For example, it may be a bottle, chair or miniature, such as an airplane, constructed to break up safely during a scene.

BUDDY FILM

A buddy film usually deals with two protagonists, traditionally male but more recently female as well. Often very different in personality, the characters usually support and complement one another either through dramatic or comedic crisis. As travel is sometimes involved in such films as a stylistic device, many buddy films are also referred to as road movies. Road movies became especially popular during the 1960s and 1970s through the success of such films as *Butch Cassidy and the Sundance Kid*, *The Sting*, *Freebie and the Bean*, *The Last Detail*, and *California Split*. Other examples of the genre are *Thelma and Louise*, *Planes, Trains & Automobiles*, and *Dumb and Dumber*. Whether a crime drama, tragedy or farce, such a film generally serves as an examination of the nature of friendship.

CANDY GLASS

Candy glass is a substance made of sugar resembling glass often used for breakaway windows and bottles. Candy glass is primarily constructed to insure safety to actors, crew, and stunt members.

CD-ROM EDITING

CD-Rom editing occurs when dailies are transferred, along with the time code, to a CD-Rom, allowing an editor instant access to any scene by simply typing in the desired time code numbers, thereby eliminating winding and rewinding film dailies or videotape reels.

CEL

A cel is a sheet of transparent cellulose acetate. These sheets are used to paint, ink, or to draw on directly, and are used for animation as well as titling. Cels have premeasured, prepunched holes, customized to the particular film ratio and animation-camera system.

Cels are put into proper registration by slipping the camera-ready cels over matching pegs on the device that hold the cels in place while they are being filmed.

CEL ANIMATION

Cel animation is film made with drawings, full art work, graphics, or abstract designs photographed or video-recorded on standardized cellulose acetate or triacetate sheets.

CINEMATOGRAPHER

The cinematographer, DP, or camera person is the individual in charge of putting the scene on film. He or she is also responsible for lighting the set or location as well as for the general composition of the scene in addition to the colors of the images, the choice of camera, lenses, filters and film stock, the setting of the camera, the integration of special effects, and the actual printing of the film.

CLICK TRACK

A click track is the metronomic beat on a sound track used by the orchestra conductor to maintain tempo for recording music after the film has been shot and edited.

COMPLETION BOND

A completion bond guarantees that principal photography on a given production will be consummated. The completion bond indemnifies the production against unforeseen costs of any sort, whether or not they resort from problems covered by insurance.

COMPUTER-GENERATED ANIMATION

Computer-generated animation refers to the technique of animating images generated by computers including scanning lines as well as the utilization of pattern-forming devices. The computer-generated images are then fed into a videotape master or transferred to motion picture film, and are especially useful for realizing otherwise difficult or expensive special effects.

COMPUTER GRAPHICS

Computer graphics is a synonym for computer-generated animation. Computer graphics also refers to specific special effects, wherein computer-generated animation is mixed with live action, titles, and credits.

CONTINUITY

Continuity refers to the development and structuring of film segments and ideas so that the intended meaning is clear. More specifically, continuity refers to the matching of individual scenic elements from shot to shot so that details and actions filmed at different times will edit together without error. This process is known as continuity edit-

125

ing. Lapses in the flow of action can be avoided by cutaways and transition devices. Likewise, music and sound are often utilized to provide a sense of continuity to a scene or sequence that may contain a variety of unmatched shots taken in different locations.

CONTROL ROOM

A control room is a soundproofed enclosure within a radio or television studio wherein the director, producer, and technicians supervise the logistics of taping or live broadcasting.

COSTUME DESIGNER

The costume designer is a person who selects or designs the clothing worn by the characters in a film, whether the period of the film is past, present, or future. He or she also oversees the production and maintenance of the wardrobe.

CRANE

A crane is a large camera trolley with a projected arm or boom at the end of which is a platform. The platform holds the camera and seats for the camera operator, camera assistant, and sometimes the director. The apparatus can move forward or backward and the arm can move up or down. Such machines are normally run electrically or hydraulically, although some are operated manually.

CROSSING THE LINE

Crossing the line entails moving the camera across an imaginary line between two or more performers so that the camera reverses its position. When shots are edited together from the different positions, the audience may lose its bearings and become confused. Screen direction may be altered by using a moving camera.

CUE SHEET

A cue sheet is a log with the sound tracks in columns that indicate to the sound engineer during dubbing where certain sounds come in and how they are to be treated when he is combining them onto a single track. The dialogue editor, the sound effects editor, and the music editor will each prepare cue sheets for the final sound mix. Footage numbers on the cue sheet correspond to those illuminated above or below the screen during image projection.

CUT

A cut refers to the splicing together of two pieces of film either to maintain continuity, change scenes, or insert other relevant material into the film flow.

CUTAWAY

A cutaway shot, edited into a scene, presents information that is not part of the first shot. It is usually followed by a return to the original shot and is often used to condense time in a scene by eliminating undesired action or to cover a loss of continuity in the action.

DAY-FOR-NIGHT PHOTOGRAPHY

Day-for-night photography is the photographic technique used to simulate night scenes that are shot in daylight. Originally created for expedience and economy, the process requires underexposure, filtration, and a careful consideration of sky conditions, color and contrast of subject and background, as well as the strength, quality, and direction of sunlight.

DAY-OUT-OF-DAYS SCHEDULE

This is a working schedule provided each day to all crew and cast members during filming. Not only is it informational, it is particularly useful to indicate scenes involving expensive actors, especially if they are contracted to work during only part of the production schedule. In that case, the actors in question should be filmed as consecutively as possible.

DIGITAL VIDEO EFFECTS

Digital video effects are produced by a software control unit with a videotape time code.

DIRECTOR

The director is responsible for interpreting the story and putting the work on film as well as for the vision and final realization of the entire motion picture.

DIRECTOR OF PHOTOGRAPHY (DP)

The director of photography (DP) is responsible for the artistic and technical quality of the screen images. Working closely with the film director to achieve optimum photographic images for the film, the DP's primary duties include selecting the camera and lighting equipment, supervising the camera and lighting crews, choosing the various lens as well as the framing of the screen image, and determining the lighting pattern, including the exposure for each scene. The most talented DPs develop a marked visual style, while the director works closely with the DP on visual compositions and moods to enhance and express the story.

DISSOLVE

The dissolve is a common gradual method of transition in which one image fades out as the other fades in. Both the end of the outgoing shot and the beginning of the incoming shot are seen on the screen simultaneously. The typical length of dissolve varies. Traditionally, a dissolve was used to indicate geographic transitions and for indicating a passage of time. The dissolve usually adds a note of finality to what has gone before. The cut, on the other hand, is usually reserved for scene continuity or for crosscutting to simultaneous action.

DOCUDRAMA

A docudrama is the story format which usually applies to made-for-television programs that present semifictionalized accounts of real or historical events.

DOLBY SOUND

Dolby Sound is a patented noise-reduction sound system that first found wide application during the 1970s and was then used in theatrical motion pictures. This sophisticated system is capable of providing high-fidelity, stereophonic-sound accompaniment on the optical sound track rather than on a magnetic tract as was once required for clear, noise-free reproduction.

DOLLY

A dolly is a mobile platform on wheels that supports the camera, camera operator, and often the assistant cameraman and allows the camera to make noiseless, moving shots in a relatively small area. The dolly grip controls the dolly's movement, which is usually on tracks.

DUB or DUBBING

Dub, or dubbing, refers to the synchronization of on-camera lip movement that replaces the existing voice, whether the actor's own, or that of another actor. This is an umbrella term for rerecording, electronic line replacement, and looping.

ECLAIR

Initially, the Eclair was the prime camera for filming synch sound documentaries in a lightweight, portable style. Its design was such that it made handheld shots easier and smoother. The Eclair was almost silent-running and its magazines could be changed in approximately ten seconds, as opposed to the several minutes it would take to change the Arriflex magazine. Today the Arriflex, Aaton, and Frezzolini magazines may be changed rapidly as well.

ELECTRONIC FIELD PRODUCTION (EFP)

Electronic field production, (EFP) utilizes lightweight, portable video gear primarily for location shooting.

ELECTRONIC NEWS GATHERING (ENG)

Electronic news gathering, (ENG) refers to on-the-spot news coverage employing highly portable videotaping systems in place of motion pictures cameras and may be used in films to simulate amateur video or news footage.

EXTREME-ANGLE SHOT

An extreme-angle shot is usually photographed from above or below, often to suggest a degree of psychological solitude of the subject, as it tends to increase the amount and importance of surrounding space and to present an unusual perspective.

FILM EDITOR

The film editor supervises the entire process of arranging and assembling the film or tape and preparing it for its final form. Working closely with the director, the film editor determines the selection, shaping, and sequence of shots, and prepares the various elements for final sound mixing and negative cutting.

FINAL CUT

The final cut refers to the last version of a film that goes into release.

FIRST ASSISTANT DIRECTOR (AD)

The first assistant director, (AD) works closely with the director as well as the production manager to organize the shooting schedule. Although the AD is primarily responsible to the director and in the execution of scheduling, he or she may assist the director with the supervision of extras, crowd scenes, and special effects. The AD also handles paperwork such as call sheets and overtime authorizations.

FISH-EYE LENS

A fish-eye lens is an extreme wide-angle lens whose glass element resembles that of a fish eye. This lens is commonly used in special effects because of its ability to distort objects at close proximity to the camera and to expand a sense of space in longer views. Utilization of this lens will cause horizons to appear to have a curved appearance.

FLASHBACK

A flashback is a scene or shot that deals with an event which has occurred prior to the film's principal time period.

FLASH-FORWARD

A flash-forward is an editing technique where scenes or shots that occur in a future time are inserted into the developing storyline of a film. Flash-forwards are often used to anticipate a critical dramatic situation or to instill a sense of mystery or danger.

FLATBED EDITING

Flatbed editing refers to the utilization of an editing machine with a horizontal bed instead of an upright working area. It contains matching pairs of circular reels, one for feedout and one for take-up. There are at least two sets of these reels, one pair for picture and one for sound.

FLOODLIGHT or FLOOD

A floodlight, or flood, refers to a type of lighting instrument as well as a quality of light. It is a lamp that disseminates a broad, nondirected area of light onto a scene. The uncontrolled quality of floodlighting may give a washed-out look to a scene but is sometimes used to create a stark visual effect.

GAFFER

The gaffer is the chief electrician, responsible for the safe and efficient execution of the lighting patterns both in the studio and on location, as indicated by the cinematographer.

GAFFER'S BEST BOY

The gaffer's best boy is the first assistant electrician.

GAUGE

The gauge of a film is measured in millimeters whose standards are 8, 16, 35, and 70 mm; 8 millimeter film has mostly been used in amateur photography, although Super 8 is now replacing the standard 8 mm film.

GENRE

Genre is a term commonly used to describe a group of motion pictures that express similar stylistic, thematic, and structural interests. For example, high concept movies such as westerns, screwball comedies, musicals, or gangster films are oten referred to as genre films.

HIGH CONCEPT

High concept films are considered to be expressed in movies such as *Jaws*, *Batman*, *Total Recall*, and *Top Gun*. High concept ideas usually have a conceptual premise and narrative that can be reduced to a catchy phrase or striking image. This film and television term has become the basis for campaigns keyed to a wave of related project merchandising.

HORIZONTAL EDITING

Horizontal editing is a system that displays A and B rolls on television screens as well as multiple camera images of a single scene. These selected takes are then combined onto a master tape.

HOT SET

A hot set is one that has been finally prepared for shooting, with scenery and props in the exact position and the lighting ready for use. Such a set should not be disturbed or even entered.

133

INTERNAL RHYTHM

Internal rhythm within a motion picture is achieved through the movement of actors or objects within a frame as distinct from external rhythms that are achieved through editing and the length of shots.

KEY GRIP

The key grip supervises all other stagehands or grips, who together assist the gaffer or chief electrician during lighting procedures and to maneuver the camera unit during moving shots. Key grips may also assist other departments in the moving and handling of equipment.

KEY MAKEUP ARTIST

The key makeup artist is head of the makeup department, responsible for the application of makeup to the film's actors. He or she coordinates directions from both director and cinematographer, and is sometimes responsible for special effects makeup as well.

LABORATORY OR LAB

A laboratory or lab is the place where film is developed and printed at various stages of motion picture production. Laboratories can also alter and improve picture quality, produce optical effects, and manufacture final release prints.

LIP-SYNC

Lip-sync is the simultaneity of a character's spoken dialogue on the sound track and lip movement in the image.

LOCATION

A location usually refers to any place other than a studio where a film is in part or completely shot.

LOCATION SCOUT or LOCATION MANGER

The location scout or location manager is the person who searches for suitable filming sites, either indoors or outdoors, which are ultimately approved by the director and other key personnel.

MATTE PAINTING

Matte painting refers to the background picture that is combined with live action, the actual set, and animated models in order to create a composite image. A matte painting may be executed on part of a glass sheet with the camera shooting through the clear area at the actual scene. Matte paintings may also be photographed from a slide for front or rear projection.

METRONOME

A metronome is a device to keep precise time. This mechanism is often utilized by film composers to establish precise tempos and sequence lengths.

MISE-EN-SCÈNE

Mise-en-scène is a French term meaning "to put into the scene." It was originally used to describe the staging of a theater director and the manner in which he arranged all the visual components on the stage, though the term has been given new life in film criticism and taken on added meaning, generally referring to the composition of the frame as well as to movement within the frame.

135

MISMATCH

A mismatch is a disorientating and seemingly illogical combination of shots where characters suddenly appear to change direction or speed and where compositional aspects of the image look unexpectedly altered. Mismatching may occur by a careless positioning of the camera from shot to shot, or by simply neglecting the proper sequential order.

MIXER or SOUND RECORDER

A mixer or sound recorder is capable of handling two or more inputs in conjunction with one common output. The term mixer is also used to describe the person in charge of balancing all the dialogue, music, and sound effects finally recorded.

MOVIOLA

Moviola is the trade name of a portable motor-driver film-viewing machine that is upright or a table variety, with the latter replacing the former. It is used for viewing but primarily for editing. Although there are numerous flatbed editing units manufactured by various companies, they are still referred to as Moviolas.

MUSIC VIDEO

This is a film or videotape of a musical recording accompanied by synchronized actions such as a dramatic interpretation of the lyrics or a series of sometimes surreal images.

NAGRA

A Nagra is a portable audio tape recorder that uses one–quarter-inch magnetic tape.

NEGATIVE CUTTING

Negative cutting is the process of editing the negative so that it exactly matches the final edited print of the film.

OFF-LINE EDITING

Off-line editing is the primary step in video editing used to make decisions about the edits in a production. The next process is usually on-line editing, or the final editing stage.

ON-LINE EDITING

On-line editing refers to reedited tapes that have been tied into the tape-mastering units for the full mix. On-line editing is also the process of making the final tape-edit, utilizing audio and video components prepared in the off-line editing sessions.

OPTICAL EFFECTS

Optical effects usually modify the photographic image filmed in a motion picture camera. Many new optical effects are now computer-generated.

OPTICAL PRINTER

An optical printer is an apparatus with an internal camera interlink, designed to make the final optical negative that may also be used for superimpositions, titling, and special effects.

OPTION

An option provides the right to make an acquisition of rights agreement by a specific time. The producer or director usually pays 5 or 10 percent of the final purchase price for the right to buy the property that may eventually become a screenplay or book for film production. Further, no one else may option or purchase the property prior to a mutually agreed upon date.

POINT OF VIEW

The term normally applies to the eyes through which we view the action. In films, the dominant perspective belongs to the neutral camera, although there are frequent divergences from this perspective to those of various characters.

POSTPRODUCTION

Postproduction is the part of filmmaking that occurs immediately after the shooting is completed and includes editing, the addition of special effects and optical transitions as well as the mixing of all sound tracks.

PRODUCER

The producer is in charge of all the financial and administrative aspects of a film production, from the inception of the film and its initial planning, through all stages of the production, distribution, and advertising.

PRODUCTION DESIGNER or ART DIRECTOR

This individual is responsible for the set design of a film. He or she works with the director and cinematographer to create settings that are compatible with other production elements so that a consistent visual style is projected for the film and to establish a special look for the picture. He or she is responsible for conceiving, planning, and supervising the overall visual design of a film.

PRODUCTION MANAGER

The production manager is the person in charge of a film's daily business and shooting arrangements. He generally starts by making a breakdown for each day's shooting, calculating the most economical way to employ performers, supervise, and tally the costs of locations as well as props.

PROPERTY MASTER

This individual is responsible for coordinating the staff of those responsible for acquiring the various props for a film. A property handler is then responsible for placing the props in the correct scenes.

REAR PROJECTION PROCESS

Rear projection process is the projection of either a still or moving picture onto the rear of a translucent screen, in front of which live action is photographed so that both the background on the screen and the foreground action are combined into a single image on the exposed film.

RERECORDING

Rerecording is the process of transferring sound from one track to another, whether from tape, from tape to magnetic film, or to an optical sound track.

RIPPLE DISSOLVE

A ripple dissolve is a type of transition that is characterized by a wavering image usually employed to indicate a change to a flashback that reflects a character's memory of an event. Sometimes, a ripple dissolve is used as a transition to an imagined event or action.

139

SCRIPT SUPERVISOR

The script supervisor is responsible for recording detailed notes regarding the shooting script during production, such as scene and take number, camera position, performance continuity, dialogue changes, and running time of each shot.

SECOND ASSISTANT DIRECTOR

The second assistant director assists the first assistant director and is responsible for much of the production paperwork as well as legwork.

SET

The set is an artificial construction used for the making of a film. A set may also convey an interior or exterior location.

SET CONSTRUCTION FOREMAN

This individual is in charge of the construction of the specially designed sets required for the film.

SET DECORATOR

The set decorator is primarily responsible for decorating and dressing the set.

SHORT-ENDS

Short-ends are the unused portion of the raw stock film that is removed from the magazine, then re-canned for possible future use or sale to raw stock outlets.

SOUND MIXER or DUBBING MIXER

This individual is in charge of mixing the various sound tracks in making the sound track master.

SPECIAL EFFECTS EXPERT

The special effects expert is head of the special effects department, responsible for the creation and coordination of the varied optical effects needed for the film.

SPOTTING

In postproduction, spotting is determining the location of music, specific dialogue, and sounds on the sound track by using a Moviola or sound reader. These decisions are usually made by the director, composer, editor, and sound effects editor.

SQUIB

A squib is a small explosive mounted to a thin metal plate, usually attached to a performer or part of a set that can be detonated by battery, wire, or remote control to suggest the impact of a bullet.

STAND-IN

A stand-in is a person with the same physical characteristics as a performer who replaces the actor or actress while the lights are set and camera position and movements are established, The stand-in enables the performer to rest, rehearse, or go about his business.

STEADICAM

A Steadicam camera is frequently used by the camera operator to move freely over rough terrain and into areas where tracks cannot be placed for a dolly.

STILL PHOTOGRAPHER

This individual is a photographer assigned to a film production for taking still pictures of actions supposedly in the film which are actually often specially staged for advertising and publicity purposes.

STORYBOARD

A visual blueprint of a film, similar to a comic strip, which represents each shot planned for the film, including additional information regarding camera movement, sound effects, etc.

STUNT COORDINATOR or STUNT GAFFER

This individual plans the safe and effective execution of the various stunts required for the film.

STUNT MAN, STUNT WOMAN

This individual substitutes for an actor or actress to perform various difficult or potentially dangerous actions.

SWEETEN

To sweeten is to add sound to an already existing track. Those sounds often include additional sound effects.

SWITCHER

In television, the switcher is in charge of electronically switching from one camera to another.

SYNCHRONIZER

A synchronizer is a device in cutting rooms for maintaining synchronization between picture and sound elements. The apparatus consists of two or more sprockets rigidly mounted on a revolving shaft or drum. Tracks are placed on the sprockets and are accurately positioned by their perforations so that they can be wound or rewound while maintaining proper synchronous interlocking.

SYNC SOUND

Usually used for dialogue, synch sound matches frame–to–frame with the picture and is especially critical in close shots. The frame-to-frame marriage of sound and picture is filmed and recorded simultaneously.

TAKE

A take is a single, uninterrupted recording of a shot. Normally, several takes are photographed for each shot and the best is used in the edited film.

TELECINE

Telecine is a device originally utilized and still used for transmitting motion pictures over television channels. Now, this helpful tool is used as well to transfer original film to videotape.

TIME CODING

Time coding is the numerical synchronization of sound and film elements encoded with matching numbers frame by frame to ensure synchronicity.

TIMING

Timing is the process of altering the density and color values of a film from shot to shot or scene to scene during printing in order to achieve consistency, balance, or some effect. These decisions are made in the laboratory by the director, timer, and cinematographer.

TRANSFER

To transfer is to copy a picture or sound being transmitted by one recorder onto another or to make a videotape reproduction from film.

TRANSITION

A transition is one of a number of devices by which a film editor moves from one scene or sequence to another. A transition usually involves a passage of time that affects the tone and flow of a motion picture. The cut, dissolve, fade-out and fade-in, washout, optical wipe, natural wipe and iris, among others, are also one of the many divisive transitions used by filmmakers.

UNIT PRODUCTION MANAGER (UPM)

The unit production manager (UPM) is responsible to the producer for assembling the budget, organizing the shooting schedule, expediting all aspects of the production, and authorizing expenditures.

VIDEOTAPE

Videotapes have a coating of magnetized iron oxide on which images and sound can be recorded for playback on television systems, either by means of a video recorder, or directly from a television transmission. Two-inch tapes were originally used for professional television recording and transmission, but have largely been replaced by one-inch tapes that can now provide equal picture quality. Three-quarter-inch tapes are often used for recording news events as well as for shooting documentaries, although the recording is transferred to wider tape for transmission. Three-quarter-inch tapes are also used as work-tapes for editing. Half-inch tapes are most popular for home use.

WARDROBE MASTER

This individual is responsible for obtaining the proper clothing, costumes, and accessories before film shooting begins.

WASHOUT

A washout is an optical transition used for editing purposes that is similar to the motion picture fade. Unlike the fade-out where the images fade to black, in a washout, the images bleach out until the screen becomes a frame of white or colored light. A new scene will then follow. Besides its use in many other films, the washout was notably used in the fantasy sequences of Catch 22 and to help create the psychological underpinning in *Cries and Whispers*.

ZOOM LENS

A zoom lens is a variable focal apparatus that can be changed from wide-angle to long-focus or the reverse. The process eliminates changing the focus or aperture setting.

STUDIES OFFERED IN FILM, TELEVISION AND VIDEO

Each of the following school entries includes the name, address, and phone number of the institution, describing its size, location, and academic calendar. In addition to indicating relevant degrees offered, information is provided concerning entrance requirements, curricular emphasis, facilities, and equipment.

As a sampling of what this country has to offer by way of film, television, and video studies, this list includes schools that offer degree programs as well as others which are geared to the working adult.

Regarding the degree programs, I have included some schools that offer traditional production studies geared toward a career in the entertainment industry, as well as institutions featuring an independent arts approach.

The facilities and equipment available may range from acceptable to outstanding. Whatever your needs, goals, or budget, there exists a program of studies for you.

Although not listed here, many community colleges offer basic film directing and video production studies. Usually, you must sign up early to be assured of a place, but such schools provide a highly accessible introduction to the craft of film directing. The author's subjective overview provides a summary of each school's offerings and approach. Inasmuch as agendas and personnel are subject to change, you are urged to contact individual schools regarding up-to-date information.

CALIFORNIA

THE AMERICAN FILM INSTITUTE
Los Angeles, CA 90027
(213)856-7600
Private two-year graduate institution.   Coed, urban location.
Graduate enrollment: 200.

CENTER FOR ADVANCED FILM AND TELEVISION STUDIES

CALENDAR: Enrollment is for the entire academic year.

DEGREES OFFERED: M.F.A.; advanced certificates.

DEPARTMENTAL MAJORS:
Graduate film and television: 28 directing; 28 producing; 28 screenwriting; 28 cinematography; 14 editing; 12 production design.

ENTRANCE REQUIREMENTS:
Graduate: transcripts; creative portfolio; summarization of prior film-
making experience; personal essay. Graduate application deadline:
February 1.

CURRICULAR EMPHASIS: Advanced courses in film and video
producing, directing, editing, cinematography, screenwriting, and
production design.

SPECIAL ACTIVITIES: Film: series/festivals; visiting lecturers;
American Video Conference; National Video Festival.

FACILITIES: 35mm, 16mm, and video-screening rooms; 16mm editing suites; video editing rooms; sound stage; film library; film research
library.

EQUIPMENT: Complete 16mm production and postproduction;
portable video equipment.

ALUMNI: David Lynch, film/TV director/writer/producer; Terrence Malick, film director; Jeremy Paul Kagan, TV/film director; Paul Schrader, screenwriter/film director; Amy Heckerling, film director; Tim Hunter, film director; Caleb Deschanel, cinematographer; Tom Rickman, film director/screenwriter; Ed Zwick, film/TV writer/director/producer; Jonathan Avnet, film/TV producer; Marty Brest, film director.

OVERVIEW: This highly professional conservatory-style school offers a one-year structured curriculum providing advanced training to Fellows who have chosen an area of specialization; second-year Fellows are chosen from first-year class; extensive internship opportunities in film and television production.

ART CENTER COLLEGE OF DESIGN
Pasadena, CA 91103
(818)396-2200
Private four-year comprehensive arts institution. Coed, urban location. Undergraduate enrollment: 1,200. Graduate enrollment: 25.

FILM DEPARTMENT

CALENDAR: Trimesters.

DEGREES OFFERED: B.F.A.

DEPARTMENTAL MAJORS:
Undergraduate film: 50 students.

ENTRANCE REQUIREMENTS:
Undergraduate: 2.5 grade point-average; ACT or SAT scores; official transcripts; portfolio required; interview recommended. Undergraduate application deadline: March 1.

CURRICULAR EMPHASIS: Film and video production with courses in cinematography, lighting, production design, directing, editing,
and writing; all forms explored, including documentary, television,
commercials, music videos, industrial and sales films, cel and computer animation, and feature films.

SPECIAL ACTIVITIES: Los Angeles film and television industry
offers sponsored assignments; placement service.

FACILITIES: 35mm screening facilities; screening room; editing
suite; sound mixing room; animation stand; permanent film library.

EQUIPMENT: Complete Super-8 and 16mm; 35mm editing equipment; portable video equipment; editing suites.

ALUMNI: Irvin Kershner, film director; Ron Osborn, film/TV
writer; Doug Claybourne, film producer; Ralph McQuarrie, special
effects artist; Steven Poster, cinematographer.

OVERVIEW: Students attending the Art Center are offered a well-
equipped professional program in film and video with an emphasis on
solid training as well as personal expression; ample exposure to both
traditional and experimental forms; many entering students have
transferred from another college; graduates are placed in production,
writing, and conceptual design areas of film/video industry; faculty of
practicing artists and designers; Art Center affiliate campus in La-
Tour-de-Peilz, Switzerland; extensive area internship opportunites.

CALIFORNIA INSTITUTE OF THE ARTS
Valencia, CA 91355
(805)255-1050
Private four-year comprehensive arts institution. Coed, suburban
location. Undergraduate enrollment: 670. Graduate enrollment: 300.

SCHOOL OF FILM/VIDEO

CALENDAR: Semesters.

DEGREES OFFERED: B.F.A., M.F.A.

DEPARTMENTAL MAJORS:
Undergraduate live action 29; experimental animation 23; character animation 159; Interschool (includes directing for theater and cinema) 3 students. Graduate live action 50; experimental animation 40; Interschool 27 students.

ENTRANCE REQUIREMENTS:
Undergraduate: portfolio; written statement of purpose. Graduate: B.F.A. degree; written statement of purpose; portfolio; production credits. Undergraduate application deadline: February 1. Graduate application deadline: February 1.

CURRICULAR EMPHASIS: Production of innovative films and videos; separate programs in experimental animation, character animation and live action; film history, theory, and aesthetics.

SPECIAL ACTIVITIES: Visiting Artists Program; student film festival.

FACILITIES: Screening room; editing suite; sound mixing room; video studio with CMX; sound stage; computer animation laboratories; motion control camera; optical printer; animation stand; film library.

EQUIPMENT: Complete 16mm and Super-8; video production and postproduction.

ALUMNI: Tim Burton, film director; John Lassiter, director/animator; Michael Pressman, film/TV director; Robert Blalack, special effects designer; Michael Patterson, music video director/writer.

OVERVIEW: Founded in 1961 by Walt Disney, Cal Arts offers degree programs in film and video production with an emphasis on innovation and an individualized course of studies; specialties in both traditional and experimental animation; faculty of practicing visual and performing artists; extensive media internship opportunities.

CALIFORNIA STATE UNIVERSITY AT LONG BEACH
Long Beach, CA 90840-2803
(310)985-4111
State four-year comprehensive institution. Coed, suburban location. Undergraduate enrollment: 26,000. Graduate enrollment: 7,000.

RADIO, TELEVISION, and FILM DEPARTMENT

CALENDAR: Semesters.

DEGREES OFFERED: B.A., radio, television, and film.

DEPARTMENTAL MAJORS:
Undergraduate radio, television, and film: 225 students.

ENTRANCE REQUIREMENTS:
Undergraduate: 2.7 grade-point average; ACT or SAT scores; interview; portfolio. Undergraduate application deadline: November 30.

CURRICULAR EMPHASIS: Electronic media theory and culture; critical film studies; media writing; audio-video-film production; media management.

SPECIAL ACTIVITIES: Film series/festivals; guest speakers.

FACILITIES: 35mm screening facilities; screening room; editing room; sound mixing room; animation stand; full video studio and editing rooms; computer graphics.

EQUIPMENT: Complete Super-8 and 16mm including CMX 6000, Callaway/Grass Valley Computerized A/B Roll; Flatbed 16mm editor; five film-cutting rooms; Aaton and Arri 16 cameras.

ALUMNI: Steven Spielberg, film/TV director/producer; Steve Martin, film actor/screenwriter; Jonathan Lawton, screenwriter/film director; David Twohy, screenwriter.

OVERVIEW: Limited enrollment to department is possible only to students enrolled at CSULB; modest budget available for student projects; department is markedly well equipped; extensive media internship opportunities.

OCCIDENTAL COLLEGE
Los Angeles, CA 90041
(213)259-2500
Private four-year comprehensive institution. Coed, urban location. Undergraduate enrollment: 17,000.

ART DEPARTMENT

CALENDAR: Quarters.

DEGREES OFFERED: B.A.

DEPARTMENTAL MAJORS:
Film and television: 40 students.

ENTRANCE REQUIREMENTS:
Undergraduate: Academic rank within top 10% of high school graduating class; competitive SAT scores. Undergraduate application deadline: February 1; April 1 for transfer students.

CURRICULAR EMPHASIS: Film study as a personal art form with experimental courses in Super-8, 16mm, and 1/2" video.

SPECIAL ACTIVITIES: Film series/festivals; film societies.

FACILITIES: Sound mixing room; screening room; editing room; sound stage; permanent library.

EQUIPMENT: Complete 16mm and Super-8; video studio and editing.

ALUMNI: Marcel Ophuls, filmmaker; Terry Gilliam, film director; George Stevens, Jr., film producer; Steve de Jarnett, film director/writer; Ken Wheat, film director; Tom Thayer, studio executive.

OVERVIEW: A selective, highly individualized program in film and television production that strongly promotes artistic and creative freedom is offered at Occidental College; cross–registration with California Institute of Technology and Art Center College of Design; media internships available for credit.

THE UNIVERSITY OF CALIFORNIA AT LOS ANGELES
Los Angeles, CA 90024
(310)825-7741
State four-year comprehensive institution. Coed, urban location.
Undergraduate enrollment: 23,000. Graduate enrollment: 12,000.

SCHOOL OF THEATER, FILM, AND TELEVISION

CALENDAR: Quarters.

DEGREES OFFERED: B.A., film and television; M.F.A., film/television production; screenwriting; animation; producers' program; M.A., Ph.D., critical studies.

DEPARTMENTAL MAJORS:
Undergraduate: 60 students. Graduate: 250 students.

ENTRANCE REQUIREMENTS:
Undergraduate: academic rank within top 12.5% of high school graduating class; 3.0 grade point-average; competitive ACT or SAT scores;
ATs in English composition, mathematics, and one additional subject
required; written portfolio. Graduate: 3.0 grade-point average; GRE
scores; personal statement; teachers' and professional recommendations; supporting materials. Undergraduate application deadline:
November 30. Graduate application deadline: November 1.

CURRICULAR EMPHASIS: Criticism; screenwriting; production;
animation. Graduate: programs in film and television production;
screenwriting; animation; critical studies; producers program.

SPECIAL ACTIVITIES: Screenings; visiting lectures; the UCLA
Film and Television Archive is the largest collection of film and video
holdings in the United States outside of the Library of Congress.

FACILITIES: Three sound stages; screening rooms; editing suites;
sound mixing rooms; animation studio; film library; film and video
archives.

EQUIPMENT: Complete 16mm; full video studio and editing.

ALUMNI: Francis Ford Coppola, director/screenwriter/producer;
Danny DeVito, director/actor; Tim Robbins, director/actor; Paul
Schrader, screenwriter/director; Penelope Spheeris, director; Neil
Jimenez, screenwriter; Alex Cox, film director; Joanna Gleason, film
director; Jeff Margolis, screenwriter.

OVERVIEW: Students in this highly ranked, well-equipped
Department of Film and Television learn history and theory as well as
the creative and technological aspects of both film and television; ani-

mation workshop program provides intensive training; all films and videos made in the department are the property of the students who have created them; extensive area internship opportunities in film and television production.

UNIVERSITY OF SOUTHERN CALIFORNIA
Los Angeles, CA 90089
(213)740-2311
Private four-year comprehensive institution. Coed, urban location.
Undergraduate enrollment: 16,000. Graduate enrollment: 12,000.

SCHOOL OF CINEMA-TELEVISION

CALENDAR: Semesters.

DEGREES OFFERED: B.A., film/video production; animation program; M.F.A., filmic writing; M.A., film/video production; M.F.A., Peter Stark motion picture producing program; graduate screenwriting; film/video production; Ph.D., critical studies; M.F.A., animation and digital art.

DEPARTMENTAL MAJORS:
Undergraduate: 400 students. Graduate: 400 students.

ENTRANCE REQUIREMENTS:
Undergraduate: 3.0 grade-point average; ACT or SAT scores; three letters of recommendation; written statement of purpose; contact Student Affairs Office for additional departmental requirements. Graduate: 3.0 grade-point average; GRE scores; three letters of recommendation; written statement of purpose; contact Student Affairs Office for additional departmental requirements. Undergraduate application deadline: February 1. Graduate application deadline: December 10.

CURRICULAR EMPHASIS: Hands-on training in all areas of production combined with critical theory and history.

SPECIAL ACTIVITIES: Series of guest speakers; special film and video screenings and retrospectives; film societies; film journals; postgraduate writing workshops.

FACILITIES: 35mm and 70mm screening facilities; screening rooms; editing suites; sound mixing room; complete animation studio; computer animation laboratory; music scoring studio; permanent video cassette/laser disc library.

EQUIPMENT: Complete 16mm; complete 8mm location; full video studio and editing; computer graphics.

ALUMNI: George Lucas, director/screenwriter/producer; Irvin Kershner, film director; John Milius, film director; Robert Zemekis, film director/writer; Randall Kleiser, film director; Les Blank, documentary film director; Laura Ziskin, film producer; William Fraker, cinematographer; Ron Howard, film director/producer; John Singleton, screenwriter/director; Dan O'Bannon, screenwriter/director.

OVERVIEW: The School of Cinema-Television was founded in 1929 and is the nation's first film school; undergraduate and graduate admissions are highly selective; the department funds some advanced projects; extensive area media internships.

FLORIDA

UNIVERSITY OF CENTRAL FLORIDA
Orlando, FL 23816
(407)823-2000
State four-year comprehensive institution. Coed, urban location. Undergraduate enrollment: 21,000. Graduate enrollment: 3,000.

SCHOOL OF COMMUNICATION

CALENDAR: Semesters.

DEGREES OFFERED: B.A., Communication.

DEPARTMENTAL MAJORS:
Undergraduate motion picture technology: 60 students.

ENTRANCE REQUIREMENTS:
Undergraduate: grade-point average of 3.0 for motion picture division; ACT or SAT scores; production credits; portfolio; written statement of purpose. Undergraduate application deadline: rolling.

CURRICULAR EMPHASIS: Students choose the production and screenwriting track or the animation track; blend of practice and theory.

SPECIAL ACTIVITIES: Film societies; classes and student productions have frequent access to nearby studios.

FACILITIES: 35mm screening facilities; screening room; 16mm editing suite; sound mixing room; animation stand.

EQUIPMENT: Complete 16mm cameras; complete postproduction; full cel and computer animation; video studio and editing.

ALUMNI: Ben Herschleder, film director/producer; Roger Donnell, film writer/producer; Jenni Gold, film producer.

OVERVIEW: Complete production training is offered through this rapidly expanding department; limited enrollment; state–of–the–art facilities in film, animation, television, and video; some production access to area studio facilities; extensive internships opportunities.

UNIVERSITY OF MIAMI SCHOOL OF COMMUNICATION
Coral Gables, FL 33124
(305)284-2265
Private four-year comprehensive institution. Coed, suburban location. Undergraduate enrollment: 8,000. Graduate enrollment: 5,000.

MOTION PICTURES DEPARTMENT

CALENDAR: Semesters.

DEGREES OFFERED: B.S., motion picture or video-film; B.F.A., communications; M.A., film studies; M.F.A., motion pictures with tracks in production and screenwriting.

DEPARTMENTAL MAJORS:
Undergraduate: 280 students. Graduate: 50 students.
ENTRANCE REQUIREMENTS:

Undergraduate: competitive grade-point average; SAT scores. Graduate: GRE scores; recommendations. Undergraduate application deadline: May 1. Graduate application deadline: April 1.

CURRICULAR EMPHASIS: The motion picture major offers tracks in producing, writing, business, or film studies; there is a video-film major with diverse curriculum; double major in College of Arts and Sciences required; most often selected second major is theater arts; graduate programs in production, screenwriting, and critical studies.

SPECIAL ACTIVITIES: Student involvement with Miami Film Festival; L.A. Spring Break Trip; Visiting Filmmaker Program; summer abroad program at the State Film School of Performing Arts in Prague.

FACILITIES: 35mm/16mm 280-seat theater; sound stage; editing suites.

EQUIPMENT: Complete 16mm and 8mm; flatbed editing; mixing theater; Oxberry animation stand; video studio and editing suites.
ALUMNI: Cynthia Cidre, screenwriter; Florie Brizel, TV/Film producer; John Pike, studio TV executive; David Isaacs, film/TV writer/producer; Andy Kuehn, media executive.

OVERVIEW: Motion Picture majors in this selective program are offered training in 16mm and 8mm film production as well as background studies in film theory and history; separate major in video-film combines curricula from motion pictures and broadcasting; extensive media internship opportunities.

ILLINOIS

COLUMBIA COLLEGE
Chicago, IL 60605-1996
(312)663-1600
Private four-year comprehensive institution. Coed, urban location. Undergraduate enrollment: 6,800. Graduate enrollment: 350.

SCHOOL OF COMMUNICATION

CALENDAR: Semesters.

DEGREES OFFERED: B.A., M.F.A., film and video.

DEPARTMENTAL MAJORS:
Undergraduate film and video: 910 students. Graduate film and video: 120 students.

ENTRANCE REQUIREMENTS:
Undergraduate: transcripts; high school diploma or GED certificate. Graduate: 3.0 grade-point average; interview; written statement of

purpose; portfolio. Undergraduate application deadline: rolling. Graduate application deadline: March 15 (fall admission only) and February 15 for international students.

CURRICULAR EMPHASIS: Intensive production training with additional offerings in critical studies, screenwriting, and management.

SPECIAL ACTIVITIES: Film series/festivals; placement assistance.

FACILITIES: Sound studio for recording, mixing, and transfer with timecode and sampling capabilities; two screening rooms with Cinemascope, laserdisc and tape projection; 12 Steenbeck editing rooms; six 3/4" off-line systems; animation studio with three Oxberry cameras; 3,300-square-foot shooting stage; film library.

EQUIPMENT: 16mm, 3/4" and Hi-band camera packages; 16mm and 3/4" off-line editing; video studio and full editing facilities.
ALUMNI: John McNaughton, screenwriter/director; Buzz Hirsch, film producer; Marcia Lamoureux, animation/filmmaker; Bill Thinnes, animator.

OVERVIEW: Columbia College offers a separate major in film and video featuring intensive studies; good access to well-equipped facilities; numerous internship opportunities.

SCHOOL OF THE ART INSTITUTE OF CHICAGO
Chicago, IL 60603
(312)899-5100
Private four-year professional arts institution. Coed, urban location. Undergraduate enrollment: 1,600. Graduate enrollment: 250.

FILM DEPARTMENT

CALENDAR: Semesters.

DEGREES OFFERED: B.F.A., M.F.A.

DEPARTMENTAL MAJORS:
Undergraduate film: 150 students. Graduate film: 25 students.

ENTRANCE REQUIREMENTS:
Undergraduate: ACT or SAT scores; art or film portfolio; written statement of purpose. Graduate: film portfolio; statement of purpose. Undergraduate application deadline: August 15.

CURRICULAR EMPHASIS: Experimental, documentary, experimental narrative, and animated film production.

SPECIAL ACTIVITIES: Film center; visiting video artists; multimedia and multi-arts performances; apprenticeships offered abroad.

FACILITIES: screening rooms; sound studio; editing suites; sound mixing rooms; transfer rooms; animation stand; computer graphics laboratory; film library.

EQUIPMENT: Complete 16mm and Super-8; Oxberry 1500 optical printer; video studio and editing.

ALUMNI: Tom Kain, film/video producer; Yvonne Welbon, film/video producer/director; Sheri Wills, film producer.

OVERVIEW: This studio fine arts institution offers degree programs stressing animation, documentary and experimental film and video forms; department encourages multidisciplinary arts interaction; personal exploration; varied internships.

SOUTHERN ILLINOIS UNIVERSITY AT CARBONDALE
Carbondale, IL 62901
(618)453-2121
State four-year comprehensive institution. Coed, rural location.
Undergraduate enrollment: 20,000. Graduate enrollment: 4,000.

DEPARTMENT OF CINEMA AND PHOTOGRAPHY

CALENDAR: Semesters.

DEGREES OFFERED: B.A., M.F.A., Cinema and Photography.

DEPARTMENTAL MAJORS:
Undergraduate cinema and photography: 300 students. Graduate cinema and photography: 50 students.

ENTRANCE REQUIREMENTS:
Undergraduate: ACT of 20 if in top quarter of high school graduating class or ACT score of 22 if in top half of graduating class; transfer credit C average. Graduate: transcripts; film portfolio; recommenda tions. Undergraduate application deadline: rolling.

CURRICULAR EMPHASIS: Department of Cinema and Photography: production, history and criticism.

SPECIAL ACTIVITIES: Big Muddy Film Festival; visiting artist lecture series.

FACILITIES: Sound stage; animation stand; screening rooms; editing rooms; sound mixing rooms; conforming rooms; film/video library.

EQUIPMENT: Complete 16mm; video studio and editing.

ALUMNI: Robert K. Weiss, film director/producer; Jim Crocker, screenwriter/producer; John Behnke, TV/film writer; Liz Ralston, special effects production; David Eubank, cinematographer.

OVERVIEW: This affordable, well-equipped department provides thorough production training; variety of internships opportunities.

MINNESOTA

FILM IN THE CITIES
St. Paul, MN 55114
(612)646-6104
State and privately supported four-year comprehensive institution. Coed, urban location. Enrollment: 600.

CALENDAR: Quarters.

DEGREES OFFERED: None; college credit as well as self–designed degree available through registration at Metropolitan State University, St. Paul.

DEPARTMENTAL MAJORS:
600 students.

ENTRANCE REQUIREMENTS:
High-school degree or equivalent. Undergraduate application deadline: rolling.

CURRICULAR EMPHASIS: Filmmaking; screenwriting; photography; audio and video production.

SPECIAL ACTIVITIES: Film series/festivals; weekend workshops with artists as part of "Lightworks" program; media access center; exhibition of independent work at movie theater.

FACILITIES: 35mm screening facilities; screening room; editing suite; sound mixing room; film library.

EQUIPMENT: Complete 16mm and Super-8; portable video cameras; VHS editing.

ALUMNI: Joel Coen, screenwriter/director; Ethan Coen, screenwriter/producer; Roger Schmitz, cinematographer; Sayer Frey, film editor.

OVERVIEW: Film in the Cities is an extremely useful resource center for those seeking access to hands-on filmmaking studies; courses and weekend workshops taught by practicing filmmakers, video artists, and screenwriters; specialized training offered for adults considering career change or wishing to design own program of studies.

NEW YORK

NEW YORK FILM ACADEMY
New York, NY 10013
(212)674-4300
Privately supported arts institution. Coed, urban location. Enrollment: varies.

CALENDAR: Basic non-sync sound course is eight weeks long; advanced sync sound course is ten weeks long.

DEGREES OFFERED: B.F.A. available through affiliated institutions.

DEPARTMENTAL MAJORS:
600 students.

ENTRANCE REQUIREMENTS:
Enrollment in basic course requires little or no experience; enrollment in advanced course requires completion of the basic course or equivalent. Undergraduate application deadline: Basic courses begin April 7; May 3; May 25; July 12; September 13. Advanced courses begin April 12; June 7; September 14; consult school for changes in schedule.

CURRICULAR EMPHASIS: Hands-on film production.

SPECIAL ACTIVITIES: Guest lecturers.

FACILITIES/EQUIPMENT: Arriflex S cameras; Arriflex BL and SR cameras; Lowell and Arri light kits; Steenbeck editing equipment.

ALUMNI: Linwood Neverson, music video director; Joe Napoli, filmmaker; Wendy Cohen, documentary filmmaker; Robert McKenna, experimental filmmaker.

OVERVIEW: This relatively new, no-frills institution, in which students are able to make films immediately in a hands-on environment, provides a practical alternative to a traditional film education.

NEW YORK UNIVERSITY
New York, NY 10003
(212)998-1212
Private four-year comprehensive institution. Coed, urban location. Undergraduate enrollment: 2,200. Graduate enrollment: 800.

FILM AND TELEVISION DEPARTMENT

CALENDAR: Semesters.

DEGREES OFFERED: B.F.A., film, video; M.F.A., film; B.F.A., M.A., Ph.D., cinema studies; B.F.A., M.F.A., dramatic writing.

DEPARTMENTAL MAJORS:
Undergraduate: 980 students. Graduate: 140 students.

ENTRANCE REQUIREMENTS:
Undergraduate: grade-point average of 3.0; ACT or SAT scores; recommendations; written statement of purpose; department requires
one-page resume highlighting creative work accomplished as well as a
nonreturnable portfolio; contact department for further details.
Graduate: transcripts; 3.0 grade–point average; portfolio; teachers'
and professional recommendations; written statement of purpose.
Undergraduate application deadline: February 1; December 1 for
early decision. Graduate application deadline: January 15.

CURRICULAR EMPHASIS: Concentrations offered in production,
writing, video, sound, photography, and animation.
SPECIAL ACTIVITIES: Directors' Series; First Run Film Festival;
Haig P. Manoogian Screenings in L.A.; student showcases; video festival; animation festival.

FACILITIES: 35mm screening facilities; three sound mixing rooms;
recording studio; digital sound postproduction facility; one Todman
sound stage plus two teaching sound stages; screening rooms; 26 editing
suites; animation stand; video studio and editing suites; film
library/archive; video studio and editing suites; computer graphics studio.

EQUIPMENT: Complete Super-8 and 16mm; complete 35mm available for graduate students.

ALUMNI: Spike Lee, film director/producer; Martin Scorsese, film
director/producer; Oliver Stone, screenwriter/director; Joel Coen,
film director; Bill Duke, film director; Martin Brest, film director;
Allan Arkush, TV director; Susan Seidelman, film director; Joel Silver,
film producer/studio executive; Amy Heckerling, film director; Chris
Columbus, film director; Alan Landsburg, TV director/producer;
Billy Crystal, film/TV actor/director.

OVERVIEW: This university offers comprehensive, quality training in film production; undergraduates may begin 35mm production in freshman year and full film/video production program in sophomore year; West Coast Alumni Group job bank matches listings and graduates; over 900 local and national media internships available at Disney Studios, MTV, HBO, and NPR, among others.

PRATT INSTITUTE
Brooklyn, NY 11205
(718)636-3600
Private four-year comprehensive institution. Coed, urban location. Undergraduate enrollment: 3,000. Graduate enrollment: 750.

MEDIA ARTS

CALENDAR: Semesters.

DEGREES OFFERED: B.F.A.

DEPARTMENTAL MAJORS:
Undergraduate: 50 students.

ENTRANCE REQUIREMENTS:
Undergraduate: ACT or SAT scores; transcripts; film, video, fine art, or photography portfolio. Undergraduate application deadline: May 15.

CURRICULAR EMPHASIS: Curriculum includes half film and half video studies composed of film and video production; history; screenwriting; cel and computer animation; there is a minor in animation.

SPECIAL ACTIVITIES: Film series/festivals.

FACILITIES: Sound mixing room; screening room; editing suites; sound stage; two animation stands; video studio; electronic editing; computer graphics suites; viewing suites; Chyron center; Quantel Paint Box; film library.

EQUIPMENT: Complete Super-8 and 16mm; video studio and editing suites.

ALUMNI: Bob Giraldi, film/TV director/producer; Steve Horn, film/TV director/producer; Jordan Levine, film editor; Aman DeFelice, special effects artist/computer graphics designer.

OVERVIEW: This highly ranked arts school offers 24-hour access to facilities; special attention to postproduction and computer video graphics; small classes taught by active professionals; students participate in a variety of film/video festivals and competitions; film and video internships.

SCHOOL OF VISUAL ARTS
New York, NY 10010
(212)592-2000
Private four-year comprehensive arts institution. Coed, urban location. Undergraduate enrollment: 2,200. Graduate enrollment: 160.

FILM/VIDEO/ANIMATION DEPARTMENT

CALENDAR: Semesters.

DEGREES OFFERED: B.F.A., M.F.A.
DEPARTMENTAL MAJORS:
Undergraduate: 275 students.

ENTRANCE REQUIREMENTS:
Undergraduate: SAT verbal 450 minimum; 3.0 grade-point average; interview; essay; portfolio. Undergraduate application deadline: rolling.

CURRICULAR EMPHASIS: Film directing; screenwriting; cinematography; editing; animation.

SPECIAL ACTIVITIES: Film screenings; industry seminars; vocational placement.

FACILITIES: Film and video editing suites; screening room; animation stands; production studios; film/video library.

EQUIPMENT: 75 Bolex and Arriflex 16mm cameras including Arri S, BL and SR; two Oxberry animation cameras; optical bench for film; two video animation systems; on-line and off-line editing; Moviola dollies

ALUMNI: Tom Sito, animator; James Muro, Stedicam operator; Michael Attanassio, TV producer; Bettiann Gishman, TV/film assistant director.

OVERVIEW: This selective arts school offers complete production training in film and video; solid animation curriculum; extensive local internship opportunites.

OREGON

NORTHWEST FILM CENTER
Portland, OR 97208
(503)221-1156
Regional media arts center. Coed, urban location. Enrollment: 1,000.

SCHOOL OF COMMUNICATION

CALENDAR: Three 15-week terms per year as well as separate semester program.

DEGREES OFFERED: B.F.A., filmmaking and animation co-offered with the Pacific Northwest College of Art; certificate program in film and video studies.

DEPARTMENTAL MAJORS:
20-25 (attending the Pacific Northwest College of Art).

ENTRANCE REQUIREMENTS:
Enrollment operates on a first-come basis. Application deadline: rolling.

CURRICULAR EMPHASIS: Hands-on production classes with professional film/video makers; short seminars and workshops conducted by visiting artists.

SPECIAL ACTIVITIES: Northwest Film Center annually sponsors three major films festivals: Northwest Film and Video Festival, for independent producers; Young People's Film and Video Festival, for kindergarten through college, held each November; Portland International Film Festival, an invitational festival held in February; touring film programs; year-round exhibition program of foreign, classic, independent, and experimental films in 480-seat Berg Swann Auditorium; video/filmmaker–in–residence program; video art installations; circulating library of films including major works of regional artists.

FACILITIES: 35mm screening facilities; screening room; editing suites; sound mixing room; animation stand; film library.

EQUIPMENT: Complete Super-8 and 16mm; video studio and edit-ing suites.

ALUMNI: Gus Van Sant, film director; Joanna Priestley, animator; John Stewart, filmmaker/director.

OVERVIEW: Classes at this lively media arts center located at the Portland Art Museum are designed for the working professional who is either already in film/video or wishes to make a career transition; access to professional equipment and hands-on experience; variety of classes; students seeking B.F.A. degree may opt for accredited semes-ter-long courses in filmmaking and animation through affiliation with the Pacific Northwest College of Art; varied internship and grant opportunities.

UNIVERSITY OF OREGON
Eugene, OR 97403-1206
(503)725-3055
State four-year comprehensive institution.   Coed, urban location.
Undergraduate enrollment: 15,000. Graduate enrollment: 4,000.

FINE AND APPLIED ARTS DEPARTMENT

CALENDAR: Quarters.

DEGREES OFFERED: B.A., B.S., B.F.A., M.F.A.

DEPARTMENTAL MAJORS: Undergraduate: 375 students. Graduate: 47 students.

ENTRANCE REQUIREMENTS:
Undergraduate: transcripts; ACT or SAT scores; letters of reference; portfolio for film students; interview recommended.   Graduate: GRE/GMAT/MAT; three letters of recommendation; transcripts;

portfolio including prior motion-graphic work for film students; statement of interest. Undergraduate application deadline: August 1. Graduate application deadline: rolling.

CURRICULAR EMPHASIS: Film/video department with an experimental arts and animation approach; developing an understanding of time as a design consideration; investigation of continuity, movement, and communication in a time-based media.

SPECIAL ACTIVITIES: Visiting artists; client projects; film societies.

FACILITIES: Screening room; editing suite; sound mixing room; animation compounds and stands; computer laboratory.

EQUIPMENT: Super-8 and 16mm cameras; editing equipment; sound recording equipment; lighting; full video studio and editing; graphics system.

ALUMNI: Uli Kretzschmar, cinematographer; Gregg Maffei, multimedia designer; Todd Kesterson, computer animator.

OVERVIEW: Experimental, animated, and documentary film production training is offered with an emphasis on individual projects.

PENNSYLVANIA

ALBRIGHT COLLEGE
Reading, PA 19612-5234
(610)921-2381
Private four-year comprehensive institution. Coed, suburban location. Undergraduate enrollment: 1,300.

ART DEPARTMENT

CALENDAR: Semesters and interim.

DEGREES OFFERED: B.A., B.S.

DEPARTMENTAL MAJORS: 25 students.

ENTRANCE REQUIREMENTS:
Undergraduate: Competitive grade point-average; ACT or SAT scores; ATs in English composition, mathematics, and a foreign language recommended; written statement of purpose; portfolio recommended; interview recommended. Undergraduate application deadline: March 15.

CURRICULAR EMPHASIS: Film/video experimental and animated production; critical theory explored in context of modern visual/fine arts media.

SPECIAL ACTIVITIES: Monthly visits by American and foreign experimental film and video artists; film series/festivals; film societies; cooperative relationship with Berks Filmmakers.

FACILITIES: Screening room; editing suite; animation stand; film and video library.

EQUIPMENT: Complete Super-8 and 16mm production and post-production; video cameras and editing.

ALUMNI: Jerry Tartaglia, experimental filmmaker; Anthony Portantino, film writer/producer; Albert Kilchesty, film executive.
OVERVIEW: Albright College offers a rigorous fine arts program that focuses on both the history and production of innovative film and video; strong visiting artist series; highly selective admissions; faculty of working media artists; production internships.

PITTSBURGH FILMMAKERS

Pittsburgh, PA 15213
(412)681-5449
Private four-year comprehensive institution. Coed, urban location.
Enrollment: 1,200.

FILM AND VIDEO PRODUCTION

CALENDAR: Semesters.
DEGREES OFFERED: B.F.A., film and video production (offered in
conjunction with Point Park College).

DEPARTMENTAL MAJORS:
70 students.

ENTRANCE REQUIREMENTS:
Determined by individual colleges and universities. Undergraduate
application deadline: determined by individual colleges and universities
.

CURRICULAR EMPHASIS: Narrative, documentary, experimental
and animated film/video productions; still photography.

SPECIAL ACTIVITIES: Pittsburgh Filmmakers operates a first–run
35mm movie theater; special screenings; showcases.

FACILITIES: 35mm screening facilities; 16mm screening room;
bench and flatbed editing suite; interlock sound mixing studio;
Oxberry animation stand; film/video library; video editing suites.

EQUIPMENT: Complete Super-8 and 16mm.

ALUMNI: John Bick, assistant film editor; Greg Funk, special effects
makeup artist; Paula Connelly, TV/Film producer; Michael Trcic,
model builder/special effects artist.

OVERVIEW: This innovative independent media arts center works in cooperation with other area schools; courses also available on a non-credit basis to independent students; encouragement of creative expression; major grant funding available.

RHODE ISLAND

RHODE ISLAND SCHOOL OF DESIGN
Providence, RI 02903
(401)454-6100
Private four-year comprehensive arts institution. Coed, urban location. Undergraduate enrollment: 2,000. Graduate enrollment: 100.

FILM/VIDEO PROGRAM

CALENDAR: Semesters and winter session.

DEGREES OFFERED: B.F.A.

DEPARTMENTAL MAJORS:
Undergraduate: 85 students.

ENTRANCE REQUIREMENTS:
Undergraduate: transcripts; SAT scores; personal statement of purpose; portfolio. Undergraduate application deadline: February 15.

CURRICULAR EMPHASIS: Production-based curriculum for artists in film, video, and animation.

SPECIAL ACTIVITIES: Film and video series/festivals.

FACILITIES: Two large shooting studios; numerous smaller studios; audio bay; editing rooms; computer workstation; two Filmmaker and one Master Series animation stand.

EQUIPMENT: Complete 16mm; full-coat audio mixing; Steenbeck 16mm editing tables; video studio and editing suites.

ALUMNI: Martha Coolidge, film director; Gus Van Sant, film producer/director; Robert Richardson, cinematographer.

OVERVIEW: A highly regarded fine arts college, Rhode Island School of Design offers visual arts students opportunities to work in film, video, and animation while refining conceptual and aesthetic skills; cross-registration with Brown University and the East Coast Art Schools Consortium; extensive local and national internships available in film and video during six-week winter session.

TEXAS

UNIVERSITY OF TEXAS AT AUSTIN
Austin, TX 78712
(512)471-3434
State four-year comprehensive institution. Coed, urban location. Undergraduate enrollment: 38,000. Graduate enrollment: 12,000.

RADIO-TELEVISION-FILM DEPARTMENT

CALENDAR: Semesters.

DEGREES OFFERED: B.S., M.A., radio/television/film; M.F.A., film/video production; M.A., screenwriting.

DEPARTMENTAL MAJORS:
Undergraduate: 600 students. Graduate: 175 students.

ENTRANCE REQUIREMENTS:
Undergraduate: grade-point average of 2.25; SAT scores. Graduate: 3.0 grade-point average; GRE scores. Undergraduate application deadline: March 1. Graduate application deadline: February 1.

CURRICULAR EMPHASIS: Production in 16mm and video; screenwriting.

SPECIAL ACTIVITIES: Film series/festivals; film societies.

FACILITIES: 35mm screening facilities; screening room; film and video editing suites; sound mixing room; film library.

EQUIPMENT: Complete 16mm; full editing.

ALUMNI: Michael Zinberg, TV/Film producer; Robert Rodriguez, film director; Cary White, set designer; Allison Gibson, writer/script editor; Wayne Lemon, writer/script editor.

OVERVIEW: Small, diverse graduate production program requires work in both film and video; writing strongly emphasized; extensive local and national internship opportunities

WASHINGTON

THE EVERGREEN STATE COLLEGE
Olympia, WA 98505
(360)866-6000
State four-year comprehensive institution. Coed, rural location. Undergraduate enrollment: 3,000.

EXPRESSIVE ARTS: FILM/VIDEO PROGRAM

CALENDAR: Quarters.

DEGREES OFFERED: B.A.

DEPARTMENTAL MAJORS: 40 students.

ENTRANCE REQUIREMENTS:
Undergraduate: Interview; recommendations; portfolio. Undergraduate application deadline: March 1.

CURRICULAR EMPHASIS: History, theory, and production of nonfiction media stressing experimental and documentary forms.

SPECIAL ACTIVITIES: Film series/ festivals.

FACILITIES: Screening room; editing suite; sound mixing room; Oxberry animation stand; JK optical printer; video studio and editing suites; film library.

EQUIPMENT: Complete Super-8 and 16mm.

ALUMNI: Matt Groening, animator/designer/writer/producer; Rhyena Halpern, film director; Michael Solinger, film editor; Lisa Farnham, film/TV producer.

OVERVIEW: This affordable state college offers an innovative interdisciplinary media arts program emphasizing nonfiction image making; development of personal forms of expression; intimate atmosphere; entry to program is competitive; all majors are student-designed; varied internship opportunities.

WISCONSIN

UNIVERSITY OF WISCONSIN AT MILWAUKEE
Milwaukee, WI 53211
(414)229-1122
State four-year comprehensive institution. Coed, urban location.
Undergraduate enrollment: 25,000. Graduate enrollment: 4,500.

DEPARTMENT OF VIDEO AND FILM

CALENDAR: Semesters.

DEGREES OFFERED: B.F.A.; M.F.A.

DEPARTMENTAL MAJORS:
Undergraduate film and video: 80 students. Graduate film and video:
15 students.

ENTRANCE REQUIREMENTS:
Undergraduate: ACT scores; portfolio. Graduate: written statement
of purpose; portfolio. Undergraduate application deadline: June 30.
Graduate application deadline: March 15.

CURRICULAR EMPHASIS: Interdisciplinary fine arts production
program in film and video stressing imaginative exploration of personal and cultural questions through experimental forms.

SPECIAL ACTIVITIES: Film series/festivals; international confer-
ences through the Center for Twentieth Century Studies on varied
topics relating to media and culture.

FACILITIES: Studio; screening room; editing suite; three multitrack
audio transfer and sound mixing studios; animation stands; Mag film
to optical sound recording; computer animation laboratory; video studio and editing suites; film archives.

EQUIPMENT: Complete 16mm including Arri Bolex, Bell & Howell; full editing.

ALUMNI: Dawn Wiedermann, filmmaker; Chris Bratton, videographer/teacher; Cathy Cook, filmmaker; Michael Collins video artist.

OVERVIEW: Students at this competitive state university are offered an interdisciplinary program emphasizing film and video production as part of a fine arts curriculum, with exposure to a variety of cinematic styles; faculty includes figures in the American and European avant-garde; production internship opportunities.

BIBLIOGRAPHY

Babchak, Richard. *New York Production Guide*. New York: *NYPG, Ltd.*, 1996.

Barbour, Alan *The Thrill Of It All*. New York and London: *Macmillan, Ltd.*, 1971.

Beaver, Frank. *Dictionary of Film Terms*. New York: *McGraw-Hill*, 1983.

Benayoun, Robert. *The Films of Woody Allen*. New York: *Harmony Books*, 1987.

Bogdanovich, Peter. *John Ford*. Berkeley: *University of California Press*, 1968.

Call, Deborah. *The Art of The Empire Strikes Back*. New York: *Ballantine Books*, 1980.

Callan, K. *Directing Your Directing Career*. Studio City: *Sweden Press*, 1995.

Ciment, Michael. *An American Odyssey*: Elia Kazan. London: *Blooomsburg Publishing, Ltd.* 1988.

Comer, Brooke. *Animation Magazine 7*. Agoura Hills, *CA Volume 7*, 1993.

Crowther, Bosley. *Hollywood Rajah, The Life and Times of Louis B. Mayer*. New York: *Holt, Rinehart and Winston*, 1960.

Edelson, Edward. *Great Movie Spectaculars*. New York: *Doubleday & Co., Inc.*, 1987.

Esquire Magazine. New York: Dec. 1996

Ederwein, Robert. *Viewer's Guide to Film Theory and Criticism*. Metuchen, NJ, & London: *Scarecrow Press*, 1979.

Eisenstein, Sergei. *Notes of a Film Director*. New York: *Dover Publications*, 1970.

Geduld, Harry. *Film Makers on Film Making*. Bloomington & London: Indiana University Press, 1970.

Goldstein, Patrick. "This Is Spinal Tap—Heavy-Metal Mania." *Los Angeles Times*: (December 18, 1983):

Goodell, Gregory. *Independent Feature Film Production*. New York: *St. Martin's Press*, 1982.

Gordon, Lester. *Let's Go to the Movies!* Santa Monica, CA: *Santa Monica Press*, 1992.

King, Larry. "Larry King Live." CNN: Los Angeles, 1996.

Koningsberg, Ira. *The Complete Film Dictionary*. New York: *Meridian*, 1987.

Lax, Eric. *Woody Allen, A Biography*. New York: *Alfred A. Knopf*, 1991.

Lee, Spike, with Ralph Wiley. *By Any Means Necessary*. New York: *Hyperion*, 1992.

Livingston, Don. *Film and the Director*. New York: *Capricorn Books*, 1969.

London, Mel. *Getting Into Film*. New York: *Ballantine Books*, 1986.

Lovell, Glenn. "The Second Lives Club." *Los Angeles Times* November 24, 1996.

Lumet, Sidney. *Making Movies*. New York: *Vintage Books*, 1996.

Maltin, Leonard. *Movie Encyclopedia*. New York: *Dutton*, 1994.

Maltin, Leonard. *The Whole Film Sourcebook*. New York: *New American Library*. 1983.

McBride, Joseph, and Douglas McVay. *The Musical Film*. New York and London: *Zwemmer Ltd.*, 1967.

McVay, Douglas. *The Musical Film*. New York and London: *Zwemmer Ltd.*, 1967.

Metcalf, Fred. *Filmmakers on Filmmaking*. Boston: *J.P. Tarcher*, 1983.

Metcalf, Fred. *The Penguin Dictionary of Modern Humorous Quotations*. London: *Penguin Books*, 1986.

Mamet, David. *The Tasks of a Director*. New York: *Penguin Books USA*, 1991.

Moore, Martha. "He's a Real Commercial Success." *USA Today*. (1993).

Obst, Lynda. *Hello, He Lied*. New York: *Little, Brown & Co.*, 1996.

Pincus, Edward, and Steven Ascher. *The Filmmaker's Handbook*. New York: *Penguin Books*, 1984.

Pintoff, Ernest. *The Complete Guide to American Film Schools*. New York: *Penguin Books*, 1994.

Silver, Alain, and James Ursini. *David Lean and His Films*. Los Angeles: *Silman-James Press*, 1992.

Stone, Drew. *Stone Films*. New York: 1996.

Silver, Alain, and Elizabeth Ward. *The Film Director's Team*. Los Angeles: *Silman-James Press*, 1992.

Silverman, Stephen. *David Lean*. New York: *Harry N. Abrams*, 1992.

Smith, John, and Tim Cawkwell. *The World Encyclopedia of the Film*. New York: *World Publishing*, 1972.

Stevenson, Ralph, and J.R. Debrix. *The Cinema as Art*. London: *Penguin Books*, 1965.

Thomas, Tony. *Film Score*. 1989. Boston: *Riverwood Press*, 1995

Thompson, David, and Ian Christie. *Scorsese on Scorsese*. New York: *Faber and Faber*, 1989.

Wiener, David. *Burns, Falls and Crashes*. Boston: *McFarland & Co.*, 1996.

Wiese, Michael. *Film and Video Budgets*. Studio City, CA: *Michael Wiese Film Productions*, 1986.

Wiese, Michael. *The Independent Film and Video Maker's Guide*. *Michael Wiese Film Productions*: Connecticut. 1984.

Youngblood, Gene. *Expanded Cinema*. New York: *E.P. Dutton & Co.*, 1970.

INDEX

M
The Mack, 80
Made-for-television programs, 129
"Magnum P.I.", 100
Major film studios, for financing films, 11
Makeup, 18, 134
Malcolm X, 71
Mamet, David, 1
Mandel, Babaloo, 72
Manduke, Joseph, 87-89
Mann, Delbert, 45
The Man with the Golden Arm, 58
Marketing, 3, 58-59. *See also* Cross-marketing
Marketing potential, 10
Marshall, Gary, 69
Marshall, Penny, 67, 69, 73
"Marty," 45
Massey, Raymond, 43
Master tape, 133
Material, selecting and acquiring, 3-8
Matewan, 73
"Matlock," 100
Matte painting, 28, 135
Matthau, Charles, 66
McCarey, Leo, 107
McCoy, Tim, 35
McNally, Terrence, 1
Melinda, 122
Menger, Sue, 65-66
Merchandising related products, 133
Messages in film, 49, 80
Method acting, 15
Metronome, 53, 135
MGM, 79
Michael, 67

R

Screen credits, 7-8, 58
Screenplays, formatting, 6
Screen tests, 20
Screenwriters' percentage, 10
Screwball comedies, 133
Scripts, centrality of, 96-97
Script supervisor, 25, 32, 41, 140
Second assistant director, 22, 66, 140
Security, 39
Sedelmaier, Joe, 47
Sena, Dominic, 49
Sequential order, 136
Set construction foreman, 21, 140
Set decorator, 32, 140
Set design, 138
Sets, 31-32, 140
    hot, 29, 133
    maintaining security on, 39
Seven, 58
Shadows, 74
Shaffer, Peter, 1
Shaft, 122
Sheppard, Sam, 1
She's Gotta Have It, 71
Shifrin, Lalo, 52
The Shoes, 48
Shooting budget, 10
Shooting schedule, 144
Shooting script, 140
Short-ends, using, 48, 140
Shot lists, 111
Shots
    cutaway, 126
    extreme-angle, 130
    sequence of, 131

Ernest Pintoff

Academy award winning director for his animated short film called *The Critic*. Ernest Pintoff lives in Hollywood with his wife, Caroline, who is a pre-school teacher and artist.

THE WRITER'S JOURNEY
MYTHIC STRUCTURE FOR WRITERS - 2ND EDITION
Christopher Vogler

This new edition provides fresh insights and observations from Vogler's ongoing work on mythology's influence on stories, movies, and man himself.

Learn why thousands of professional writers have made THE WRITER'S JOURNEY a best-seller which is considered "required reading" by many of Hollywood's top studios! Learn how master storytellers have used mythic structure to create powerful stories which tap into the mythological core which exists in us all.

Writers of both fiction and nonfiction will discover a set of useful myth-inspired storytelling paradigms (i.e., *The Hero's Journey*) and step-by-step guidelines to plot and character development. Based on the work of Joseph Campbell, THE WRITER'S JOURNEY is a must for writers of all kinds.

New analyses of box office blockbusters such as *Titanic*, *The Lion King*, *The Full Monty*, *Pulp Fiction* and *Star Wars*.

First released in 1993, THE WRITER'S JOURNEY quickly became one of the most popular books on writing in the past 50 years. New material includes:

• A foreword describing the worldwide reaction to the first edition and the continued influence of THE HERO'S JOURNEY Model.
• Vogler's new observations on the adaptability of THE WRITER'S JOURNEY for international markets, the changing profile of the audience.
• How to apply THE WRITER'S JOURNEY paradigm to your own life.

$22.95, ISBN 0-941188-70-1
300 pages, 6 x 8 1/4
Order # 2598RLS

CALL 24 Hours A Day
1-800-833-5738

FILM DIRECTING
SHOT BY SHOT
Steven Katz

Every page in this international best-seller is loaded with career-saving information for both first-time directors and seasoned pros. It is filled with visual techniques for filmmakers to expand their stylistic knowledge. With beautiful illustrations and expertly written directions, *Shot by Shot* has been used as a reference tool "on the set" by many of Hollywood's directors.

Provides insight into the work of Spielberg, Welles and Hitchcock with many **never before published** storyboards for *Empire of the Sun, Citizen Kane, The Birds*. If you read no other film book, read this one!

"...helps (students) move the film that's in their head to paper and communicate it to their actors and crew..."
> **Professor Fred Watkins**, University of North Texas
> Department of Radio TV Film, Denton, Texas

"...an excellent text for teaching students how to visualize the flow of shots in a scene and how to incorporate storyboards into preproduction."
> **Professor Duane Meeks**, Regent University
> School of Cinema Television

A Doubleday Stage & Screen Book Club Selection

$24.95, 370 pages, 7 x 10, 750+ illus.
ISBN: 0-941188-10-8
Order # 7RLS

The Independent Film & Videomaker's Guide
–2ND EDITION
Michael Wiese

Wiese has packed 25 years experience in film and video into the most comprehensive and most useful book ever for filmmakers seeking both independence and success in the marketplace. Loaded with insider's tips to help filmmakers avoid the pitfalls of show business, this book is the equivalent of a "street smart degree" in filmmaking.

This new, completely expanded and revised edition has all the information you need from raising the cash through distribution that caused the original edition to sell more than 35,000 copies.

Contents include writing mission statements, developing your ideas into concepts, scriptwriting, directing, producing, market research, the distribution markets (theatrical, home video, television, international), financing your film, pitching, presentations, writing a business plan, and a huge appendix filled with film cash flow projections, sample contracts, valuable contact addresses, and much more.

> *"A straightforward and clear overview on the business of making films or videos. Wiese covers the most important (and least taught) part of the job: creative deal-making. The book is full of practical tips on how to get a film or video project financed, produced, and distributed without sacrificing artistic integrity. A must for any aspiring independent producer."*
> **Co-Evolution Quarterly** (about the first edition)

$29.95, Approx. 500 pages, over 30 illustrations, 6 x 8 1/4, ISBN 0-941188-57-4, Order # 37RLS

On Sale September 1998

To order this book for classroom use, please call Focal Press at 1-800-366-2665.

MICHAEL WIESE PRODUCTIONS

11288 Ventura Blvd., Suite 821
Studio City, CA 91604
1-818-379-8799
kenlee@earthlink.net
www.mwp.com

Write or Fax
for a
free catalog.

Please send me the following books:

Title   *Order Number (#RLS___)*   *Amount*

_____ _____

_____ _____

_____ _____

_____ _____

SHIPPING   _____

California Tax (8.25%)   _____

TOTAL ENCLOSED   _____

Please make check or money order payable to
Michael Wiese Productions

(Check one) ___ Master Card ___Visa ___Amex

Credit Card Number_____

Expiration Date_____

Cardholder's Name_____

Cardholder's Signature_____

SHIP TO:

Name_____

Address_____

City_____State_____Zip_____

HOW TO ORDER
**CALL
24 HOURS
7 DAYS A WEEK**

**CREDIT CARD
ORDERS
CALL
1-800-833-5738**

OR **FAX YOUR
ORDER
818-986-3408**

OR **MAIL THIS
FORM**

SHIPPING
ALL ORDER MUST BE PREPAID
UPS GROUND SERVICE
ONE ITEM - $7.00
EACH ADDTLN ITEM, ADD $2

SPECIAL REPORTS - $2 EACH.
EXPRESS -3 BUSINESS DAYS
ADD $12 PER ORDER

OVERSEAS
SURFACE - $15.00 EACH ITEM
AIRMIAL - $30.00 EACH ITEM